THE SUNNI AND THE SHĪ'A:

History, Doctrines and Discrepancies

Abdul Ganiy Oloruntele

TRUE DIRECTIONS
AN AFFILIATE OF TARCHER PERIGEE

iUniverse®

THE SUNNI AND THE SHĪ‘A:
HISTORY, DOCTRINES AND DISCREPANCIES

iUniverse books may be ordered through booksellers or by contacting:

iUniverse
1663 Liberty Drive
Bloomington, IN 47403
www.iuniverse.com
1-800-Authors (1-800-288-4677)

ISBN: 978-1-5320-0970-9 (sc)
ISBN: 978-1-5320-0971-6 (e)

Print information available on the last page.

iUniverse rev. date: 10/29/2016

بسم الله الرحمن الرحيم

In the name of Allah, the Most Compassionate, the Most Merciful

And hold fast, all of you, by the Rope (Islam) which Allah (stretches out for you) and be not divided among your selves; and remember with gratitude Allah's favour on you; for you were enemies and He joined your hearts in love, so that by His grace, you (all) become brothers (of the same faith).

Āl-Imrān 3:103

And obey Allah and His Messenger; and fall into no disputes, lest you lose courage and (then) your strength (or power) departs; and be patient (with one another): For Allah is with the patient ones.

al-Anfāl 8:46

Dedication

This work is dedicated to Almighty Allah, the only one who guides us towards the right path.

It is also dedicated to my late father, Imam Abdul Qadir Oloruntele, who devoted most of his life to working for the unity of all Muslims in his locality. May Allah grant him everlasting forgiveness, and *al-Jannah*.

Acknowledgements

Praise and thanks be to Almighty Allah, Lord and Cherisher of the whole world. May His everlasting peace and blessings be upon our holy Prophet Muḥammad, his household, his companions, and all sincere Muslims of all generations, until the end of time.

I would like to express my profound gratitude to my teachers/tutors in Nigeria. Their contributions to my academic success afforded me the background that enabled me to write for *The Sunni and the Shīʿa: History, Doctrines, and Discrepancies*. These eminent personalities include the following:

Sheikh Abdullah Abdul-Hameed, the chief Imam Imale of Ilorin; Sheikh Waliyullah Aliy-Kamal (formerly of Kwara State College of Education, Ilorin); Sheikh Abdul-Lateef Adekilekun (formerly of Kwara State College of Education, Ilorin); the late Sheikh Musa Adeleke Ahmed (formerly of the Kwara State College of Education, Ilorin); Professor Hamzat I. Abdul-Raheem, Kwara State University, Ilorin; Professor Ishaq O. Oloyede, former vice chancellor, University of Ilorin; Professor Adedayọ Yusuf Abdul-Kareem, University of Ilorin; Dr ʿAbdus-Samīʿi Imam Arikewuyo, Kwara State University, Ilorin; Dr Ibrahim S. Katibi; and the late Sheikh Ameenullah Ibraheem

I appreciate the advice and encouragement of the following people: Dr Ishaq Ibrahim Ọlayiwọla, Ibrahim Badamasi Babangida University, Lapai; Abdul-Ganiy Adebayọ Alabi, Federal College of Education, Okene; Moshood A. Hadi; Abdul-Ganiy Abdullah; Abdul Hafeez Ameen-Ibrahim; Kwara State College of Education, Ilorin; Dr Sulaiman

S. Adua, Kwara State University, Ilorin; Muhammad F. Abdul-Salam, Ọlọrunshogo Generation Company, Shagamu; Ismaila O. Oboh, National Bureau of Statistics, Calabar; Abdul-Rafi'i Agboọla, Trust Computer, Oṣogbo; Imam Haroon Salman Ayinla; and Alhaj Usman Bayọ Arẹmu.

I am indebted to my teacher and supervisor in the United Kingdom, Dr Jabal Muhammad Buaben, formerly of the University of Birmingham. I equally value the encouragement of the following friends: Dr Waheed O. Azeez, Education Officer, UNISON, Oxleas branch, London; Mohadi Issaka; Muhammad Bello Tirmidhiy, Bemut Tutors, London; Taofeeq Kareem, manager, Throne Recruitment Agency, Birmingham; and Abdullah Sanni, Fareed Sheikh Chartered Accountant, Ontario, Canada. I thank my son, Abdul Roqeeb, who typed the manuscript.

To all of those mentioned *jazākumullāhu khayra*.

Contents

Introduction

Out of the 1.7 billion Muslims in the world today, over a billion are Sunni Muslims. That is why they are called the Sunni majority, whereas the others are considered to be the Shi'ite minority.

It is amazing to consider that a large percentage of Muslims do not know why they are called either Sunni or Shīʿa. The numerous Muslim factions today each fall under one of the two dominant bodies. Why do the Sunni, led by Saudi Arabia, and the Shīʿa, led by Iran, turn out to be staunch antagonists when they are all followers of the same Islam?

The conflicts between these two factions are definitely affecting world peace today. Muslims and non-Muslims alike know the two factions as rivals and staunch antagonists that wage unnecessary wars against each other.

Who are the Sunni, and who are the Shīʿa? What is the origin of each faction, and what is the cause of their seemingly unending enmity? What doctrines have they in common, and what are their discrepancies? Have the two ever made any effort to reconcile? If they had, then why do they still oppose one another? And if they have made no effort, then is this how Muslims will continue until the end of time? All of these questions are what *The Sunni and the Shīʿa: History, Doctrines, and Discrepancies* intends to discuss in brief. The main aims and objectives are to (*a*) enlighten the English-speaking Muslims about the origin of Muslim disunity; (*b*) establish the discrepancies between Sunnism and Shiʿism as being partly the result of unavoidable natural differences in humanity and partly the result of egocentric interests; (*c*) make it plain that each individual Muslim sees his or her views, opinions, and beliefs as being the best and the most correct; (d) affirm that, despite the discrepancies, it is still possible through tolerance, for Sunnis and Shīʿas to become genuine brothers and sisters of the same faith.

This is expected to lead educated Muslims to broaden their minds and tolerate one another so as to finally attain internal unity and security, thereby preventing Sunni vs. Shīʿa aggression. It is hoped that this effort will have a positive impacts on the attitudes of Muslims across the world.

The Sunni and the Shīʿa: History, Doctrines, and Discrepancies is a continuation of the themes and ideas presented in the author's book *ʿIlm al-Kalām: The Science of Dialectic Theology* with *the History and Doctrines of the Early Muslim Sects*. Of course, many authors and researchers have written about the Sunni and about the Shīʿa. However, insights applying to both factions have not been combined as they are in *The Sunni and the Shīʿa* in such a way that suits the taste of not only academics but also the general public. The present author looks at each faction of Islam through the lens of its respective beliefs and documents, also considering the works of some non-Muslim authors. It is hoped that *The Sunni and the Shīʿa* will be useful to students and teachers of Islamic studies in every English-speaking institution of learning across the world.

May Allah continue to shower His unending mercy and blessings upon the holy Prophet Muḥammad, his household, and his companions, and upon the sincere Muslims of every generation, until the end of time.

Chapter 1

The Sunni

Preamble: Historical Context and Reasons for Division

In the presence of thousands of followers, Prophet Muḥammad (pbuh) delivered his last sermon, in which he warned Muslims of all generations against division and its consequences. He said that Muslims should not stray from the path of righteousness; should hurt no one (so as not to be hurt by others); should regard their lives and property as sacred, and not destroy either; should regard themselves as the brother (or sister) of every other Muslim; should acknowledge that no one is superior to the another except in piety; should remain united; and should not be divided. Unfortunately, this advice and these warnings were pushed aside after the Prophet died. This was done as a result of the following factors:

a) The natural differences among human beings

As intelligent as human beings are, more intelligent than any other creature, they are naturally created to view a single issue in various ways on account of the variation in their intelligence, wisdom, knowledge, and life experiences. Muslims are no exception to this rule.

b) The allegorical nature of some Qur'anic verses

The Holy Qur'an confirms that some of its verses are allegorical (having different interpretations) and indicates that some others are ambiguous or obscure in their meaning (*Āl-Imrān* 3:7). It is mentioned above that a single issue which is not ambiguous is viewed or perceived differently by different people, never mind an issue which is ambiguous.

The Holy Qur'an urges Muslims to have strong faith in some phenomena which are invisible (e.g. God, His attributes, the angels, jinn, Paradise, Hell, free will, predestination). The apparent phenomena in our physical world are interpreted and understood differently by different people, so it is not surprising that invisible phenomena are understood differently by different people. It is obvious that invisible phenomena will inspire varying views, opinions, beliefs, explanations, interpretations, and understandings. This is one of the things that accounts for the past and present divisions among Muslims.

c) Tribal or racial sentiment

Naturally, human beings tend to be loving towards and loyal to their own people (people of the same blood, tribe, or race), sometimes to the detriment of others. This explains why the Madīnans clamoured for their own indigene as a leader, and why the clan of the Prophet and 'Ali ibn Abi Ṭālib, Banū Hāshim, delayed their recognition of Abu Bakr as the first caliph despite his popularity among the early Muslims. Instead, the clan of the Prophet backed their own son 'Ali as the most suitable candidate. And the Umayyad clan were so in favour of 'Uthmān ibn 'Affān that they dominated the political aspect of the caliphate. This type of racial sentiment has today extended to manifest as state or national patriotism. It was reflected in the past and is manifest today, as seen in Muslim nations that forgo the concept of Islamic brotherhood when it comes to defending or protecting their racial or national interests.

d) Political interest

The above three reasons were enough for the looming divisions between Muslims, but the most crucial factor which accounted for Muslim division, especially concerning Sunni and Shīʿa, was power struggle. The issue transformed from political rifts to personality clashes, and later to theological conflicts. The Sunni are mostly concerned with theological concepts, whereas the Shīʿa concentrate on personalities.

In fact, when the Prophet's leadership was centred in Madīnah, a few companions led by Abdullāh ibn Ubayy envied the Prophet and even schemed to force the Prophet and his Makkan followers (the Muhājirūn) out of Madīnah (*al-Munāfiqūn* 63:7–8). The impact of this small group was not felt thanks to the leadership style of the Prophet, his charisma, and other superlative qualities naturally endowed to him.

Immediately after Prophet Muḥammad's death, the political struggle regarding who should be the next leader resurfaced. This temporarily divided Muslims into three main groups. The majority favoured the childhood friend of the Prophet, Abu Bakr Ṣiddīq, because there were indications from the Prophet which pointed to his election.

But other indications from the Prophet pointed to one of his cousins, ʿAli ibn Abi Ṭālib, who had married the Prophet's only surviving daughter. Therefore, ʿAli had his own faction and supporters, consisting especially his tribespeople (Banū Hāshim) and his close associates.

The third group consisted of some Madīnans who wanted a leader from among their tribespeople. This division had little effect thanks to the personality and leadership style of Abu Bakr. Two other eminent personalities, ʿUmar ibn al-Khaṭṭāb and ʿUthmān ibn ʿAffān, were elected before the caliphate finally went to ʿAli.

> Of course, other motives might have been present, but the most glaring factor which caused the first and second civil wars among Muslims was political interest. Unfortunately, the two civil wars broke out during the caliphate of ʿAli b. Abi Ṭālib. In addition, the first ever sect of Muslims separated from ʿAli's original supporters and formed an independent group called the Khawārij (Khārijites). This was the group responsible for ʿAli's death.

Since those times, various political and/or theological groups, sects, and factions continued to develop. The proliferation was so great at one time that some Muslim scholars and a few political leaders decided to shoulder the responsibility for reuniting all the factions. The effort lasted for centuries. Ultimately, through tolerance, they were able to secure their unity and internal security in order to fight against external aggression under one umbrella of Islamic brotherhood.

If these various Muslims factions had at a point in time reunited as one, then who are the Sunni and who are the Shīʿa? Was there any sect or faction originally known as Sunni? How did this faction come about and then go on to dominate all other sects and groups? What is the meaning of the name Sunni? And what are the general beliefs which separate the Sunni from the Shīʿa? These are some of the questions that will be discussed in this chapter.

In any event, regarding all of the above *fitnah* (troubles including civil wars and breaking into numerous factions) that occurred during this early period, it is very difficult for any researcher or writer to discover the exact truth of any of the matters in question. This is because each faction wrote the history in its own favour and cast the blame onto its opponents. An objective writer, therefore, needs to consult source documents of various factions to move closer to the truth.

Articulation of Sunnism

It should be stated here, as alluded to above, that Muslim sects were once so numerous that compiling a list of them would result in a moderate-sized pamphlet. In fact, each larger sect subdivided into so many smaller sects that mentioning each of them here would render this section of *The Sunni and the Shīʿa* boring and monotonous. It is fair to say, however, that on account of rivalry between, and the battle for survival of, these numerous sects, the Islamic Empire was marked by not only hatred and chaos but also many revolts, forgeries, lies, unnecessary condemnations, and even wars. All of these things eventually led to internal insecurity and external threat.

It should be recalled that as early as 38 AH/658 CE, the first Muslim sect, Khawārij (the Khārijites), was already in existence, calling every Muslim *kāfir* (unbeliever) for not believing in their new doctrines, especially the Azraqite faction among them. Thus, if such excommunication of one another from the fold of Islam had started at this early period, if Muslims had waged wars against one another, taking several thousands of lives fewer than thirty years after the Prophet's death, then one can imagine the situation of Muslims one hundred years later.

The situation was a complicated one, with various sects struggling for power, recognition, and survival, including the then existing *madhhabs* (schools of jurisprudence), as one school was, at times, favoured above the others by some Umayyad and Abbasid caliphs. This led to frequent acts of hatred, riots, bloodshed, and the burning of mosques and *madāris* (schools).[1] Each time a group of Muslims divided into a new sects, new names, beliefs, and/or doctrines surfaced as a result, with each sect believing itself to be the best group with the most authentic practice of Islam.

In order to solve these compounded problems and attain unity and security throughout the Muslim lands, Islamic scholars decided to take practical steps. The efforts were successive ones that lasted for centuries, between 750 CE and 950 CE. They included laying down basic rules for some of the important affected branches of Islamic knowledge, tolerating the opinions and doctrines of all sects that were believed to be rightly guided, and gradually eliminating those sects considered to be on an errant path. Of course, a few caliphs provided considerable political assistance for these efforts, but Islamic scholars were the parties responsible for putting forth the greatest effort to reunite Muslims. Writing of this period, William Montgomery Watt asserted, 'The main background of Sunnism was the insecurity from fighting of all factions and revolts in many areas. In so far as men felt that establishment of Sunnism will give them security, they wanted to see further consolidations [of the various Muslim sects].'[2]

Section 1
Codification of Islamic Sciences

Based on the background provided in the foregoing preamble, we will now summarise the problematic situation of each affected branch of Islamic knowledge, as well as discuss other doctrines, before explaining the scholars' resolutions and their efforts to codify Sunnism as a whole.

Hadith (Prophet's Traditions)

The Holy Qur'an has, all along, remained as a single book and a binding force for all Muslims regardless of their sectarian affiliation. Next to it is the Hadith, which Sunni and Shīʿa perceive differently. It is necessary to discuss the codification of the Hadith first, as the efforts made on other branches of knowledge and Sunni theology rely on the Hadith.

Right from the start of the revelation, the Prophet's explanations, responses to questions, clarifications of issues, warnings, and practical demonstrations, and his companions' descriptions of his personality, here known as Hadith, had always been considered as being second to the Holy Qur'an. There was no disagreement among Muslims regarding this status of the Hadith. Scholars and political leaders always felt confident quoting from the Hadith to provide support for any of their actions.

However, along with the problematic situations brought about by the numerous divisions among Muslims, Hadith fabrications became rampant, which greatly disturbed Islamic scholars. As early as the period of the conflict between 'Ali and Mu'āwiyah, spurious traditions started to surface for the purpose of settling political scores. 'It seems as if the first fabrication began in the political sphere, crediting and discrediting the party concern.'[3] Ibn Abi al-Ḥadīd, as quoted by Aḥmad Amīn, traced a forgery of the Hadith to the time of the death of the Prophet. This forgery was the work of the supporters of 'Ali, who were against Abu Bakr.[4]

In one report, Muhammad Muhsin Khan explains that Imam Bukhāri collected over three hundred thousand Hadiths, of which he 'memorized 200,000, of which some were unreliable. He was born at a time when Ḥadīth was being forged either to please rulers or kings or to corrupt the religion of Islam'.[5]

In another report about Imam Bukhāri, this one made by Ibn Hajar, it is reported that Bukhāri collected 600,000 Hadiths. He selected only 7,397 traditions that were repeated under various headings, and only 2,602 traditions without repetitions.[6] This means, according to Alfred Guillaume, that fewer than one out of every two hundred traditions during Bukhāri's time could pass his test of authenticity.[7] 'There is no dispute over the occurrence of extensive forgery in Ḥadīth literature. The 'Ulama' of Ḥadīth are unanimous on this, and some have gone so far as to affirm that in no other branch of Islamic science has there been so much forgery as in Ḥadīth.'[8] According to Muḥammad Ṣiddīqī, former professor of Islamic culture, 'All the Islamic authorities agree that enormous amount of forgery was committed in the ḥadīth literature. Imām Aḥmad ibn Ḥanbal has said that ḥadīth and *tafsīr* have been more affected by forgery than any branch of literature.'[9] Guillaume continues along these lines, asserting, 'So many traditions are demonstrably false, so many can be proved to be later origin … many are obviously of foreign origin, particularly Jewish, and in a lesser degree Christian.'[10]

In short, for the purpose of providing themselves with political or doctrinal support, or for other reasons, different people embarked on fabricating Hadiths. 'Some of them were heretics', says Dr Abu Ameenah Bilal Philips, 'even Muslims, especially the illiterate ones engaged in forgery for genuine intention, especially to defend their various doctrines or dogmas. In fact, for a fabricator to be trusted he will have to relay some true Ḥadeeths along with his fabrications.'[11]

Despite the fact that Ibn al-Ṣalāḥ al-Shahrazūrī, Muhammad 'Ajjāj al-Khaṭīb, Muhammad Musṭafa A'zami, Abu Ameenah Bilal Philips, Scott C. Lucas, and Muhammad Zubayr Ṣiddīqī (among others) have all produced outstanding works explaining and defending the Hadith, all of these writers nevertheless accept that some Hadiths were forgeries. Still, they all discuss the rigorous and brilliant efforts of the early scholars to compile the authentic Hadiths.

Given the fact that some Hadiths were forged, it is obvious that scholars have enormous tasks ahead of them. In order to detect the forgeries among the true Sunnah, they divided all of the compiled Hadiths into numerous categories.[12]

In the early days of Islam, leading scholars of different regions, especially the jurists (*fuqahāh*), collected various Hadiths to use in coming to Islamic legal verdicts. The Muwaṭṭa' collection of Hadiths was already in use by Imam Mālik, and other scholars in other regions had their own collections. Some traditions known to people in Makkah were unfamiliar to the people in Madīnah, even though these two cities are near to each other in the Ḥijazi region. Imam al-Shāfi'i said that out of the many Hadiths available for *uṣūl al-aḥkām* (basis for legal rulings), his teacher Imam Mālik in Madīnah had only thirty with him, whereas his other teacher, Sufyān ibn Uyayna in Makkah, had sixty.[13]

The same was the case in other areas, such as Kufa, Basra, Baghdad, and Damascus. This means that 'the collection of Hadith was carried on from the beginning and so for a long time as a private concern'.[14] And this practice had a temporary negative impact on other fields of Islamic science, like *fiqh* (Jurisprudence), *tafsīr* (Qur'an exegesis), and *tajwīd* (Qur'an recitation), because specialists in these sciences relied on Hadiths yet to be tested and trusted, as will be discussed shortly. This was one of the reasons why a few scholars used to change their verdicts when they came across more authentic Hadiths.

Many Hadith specialists took upon themselves the responsibility of putting all of the Hadiths of these various centres together. Many Hadith collections came into existence as a result.

Without forgetting the fabrication problem, these scholars laid down strict general rules and regulations for determining the authenticity of the Hadith. According to Ibn al-Qayyim, as quoted by A'zami,[15] any Hadith would be rejected if it:

- contained an exaggerated statement;
- contradicted a well-established Sunnah;
- consisted of a saying which was supposed to have been made in the presence of hundreds of companions, but (it is claimed) all of them concealed it;
- consisted of a saying or Hadith that had no resemblance to all other statements of the Prophet;
- contradicted any obvious meaning of the Qur'an;
- was inadequate in style;
- was against reason, the law of nature, or common experience;
- contained the dates and details of future events; or
- stated the superiority of virtue of a person, tribe, or place.

The above rules applied to the content or report of any saying, deed, or action of the Prophet. Alongside this effort, scholars also compiled the biographies of the transmitters, and then emphasised the strict use of *isnād*, which was already in existence but not previously applied. That is, the scholars compiled the names and biographies of each Hadith transmitter from the companions up to their own generation.[16] Thus, with this effort they were able to distinguish between transmitters of each generation who were either honest or liars, or those known for their retentive memories versus those who had weak memories.

As a result of the effort (encouraged by the scholars) to collect all Hadiths together from different localities and across numerous regions, different collections began to surface from various specialists. Many of these specialists had travelled widely throughout all Muslim lands in search of Hadith. But when the strict guidelines regarding the Hadiths, their transmitters, and the compilers' (who were their contemporaries) methods of compilation were applied, many Hadith collections were determined not to be up to the set standard.[17] Only five, compiled by the following personalities, were initially graded as the best: Bukhāri, Muslim, Abū-Dāwūd al-Sijistānī, Nasāʾī, and Tirmidhī.[18] Ibn Mājah's collection was later added to these five. These six are named *ṣiḥāḥ sittah*, the six authentic books of Hadith.

The early scholars were strict. Imam Bukhāri and Imam Muslim were students of Imam Aḥmad ibn Ḥanbal, who recorded thirty thousand of the millions of Hadiths. As venerated as Ibn Ḥanbal was, his collection (*musnad*) was placed in the ungraded category. This does not mean, however, that authentic Hadiths are not found in any of the ungraded collections. Far from it, as the six rated collections do not completely record the authentic Hadiths speaking to all aspects of life.

These scholars' great efforts were appreciated and accepted by the majority of the early Muslims of all factions except the Shīʿa, who were adamant that only Hadiths from ʿAli b. Abi Ṭālib and his family should be accepted. Hence, they compiled and codified their Hadiths separately, relying occasionally on the Sunni collections if any Hadith therein was in support of their doctrines. One of their reasons for this was that only *Ahl al-Bayt* (ʿAli and his descendants) and a few companions of the Prophet who sincerely stood by ʿAli were credible in their reports about the Prophet. As long as others were, to them, not credible, any report from those others could not be taken as credible.

Therefore, all Muslims, known then as *Ahl al-Sunnat wa'l-Jamāʿah*, accepted the grading of the six sound collections of Hadith as the most authentic. The Sunni scholars were able to achieve unity of all Muslims of every generation and every locality based on these ratings.

Al-Muwaṭṭaʾ of Imam Mālik was not rejected. It contains collections of genuine Hadiths, companions' opinions, and personal verdicts based on the early customs of Madīnah. All the Hadiths in al-Muwaṭṭa' are confirmed by Bukhāri and Muslim.[19] This is why some scholars have ranked it among the six authentic collections.

Tafsīr (Qur'an Exegesis)

The Holy Qur'an was revealed with great richness in its meanings, so rich that Allah confirms that no one knows the totality of the Qur'an's meaning except Him alone (*Āl-Imrān* 3:7). This is why the Qur'an needs extensive interpretations and explanations of its meanings, which are here known as *tafsīr*.

Of course, many of the Prophet's companions, some of whom were more gifted in Qur'anic interpretation than others, were witnesses to the Qur'anic revelations and the reasons behind these revelations. As the Islamic Empire expanded after the Prophet died, learned *ṣaḥābah* settled in the various conquered regions. For instance, 'Abdullāh b. 'Abbās remained in Makkah and produced many competent scholars[20] among the *tābi'ūn* (followers of the companions who did not meet the Prophet or who were young when the Prophet died and so didn't remember him well). Ubayy Ibn Ka'b had students[21] gathered around him in Madīnah, while 'Abdullāh b. Mas'ūd settled in Iraq and also produced notable scholars.[22] Since their students (*tābi'ūn*) did not witness the revelations, naturally they had to answer questions and provide clarification regarding the rationale behind some of the revelations. In addition, because 'the depth of comprehension of the Qur'aan's meaning will vary from the individual to individual due to natural differences in intelligence',[23] explanations of the Qur'an's language style and of all the divine laws were essential.

All these factors led to the rapid development of *tafsīr*, which had already begun to be gradually developed during the Prophet's time. 'Even before the whole of the Qur'aan was revealed, people used to ask the Apostle all sorts of questions as to the meaning of certain words in verses revealed.'[24] Subsequently, the following generations received more and more extensive explanations of the Holy Qur'an from previous generations.

It is self-evident that the Qur'an has been perfectly protected from any sort of distortion or corruption. Interpreting the Qur'an by referring to other verses within it was not a problem. The whole Book was then, as it still is, intact. However, because of the many divisions among Muslims, which led to various doctrines; the conversion of non-Muslims to Islam; the introduction of Greek philosophy; the evolution of the Arabic language with the introduction of more foreign vocabularies and the loss of some of the original vocabulary; and the forgery or distortion of the Prophet's sayings and actions – among other things – it became glaringly unavoidable that the true interpretations of the Qur'an had to be safeguarded.

According to Yusuf Ali, it was then 'necessary to establish strict rules by which the evidence could be examined and tested, so as to separate that which was considered to be established from that which was doubtful or weak, and that which was to be rejected as unproved'.[25] In their efforts to codify the Hadith, as discussed earlier, scholars noted the unavoidable human differences in the companions. It became clear that some had more retentive memories than others, some had better access to the Prophet than others, some had deeper language aptitude than others, and so forth.

Thus, given all of the above factors, scholars applied strict rules to the Hadith literature to compile all Hadiths consistent with the interpretation of the Holy Qur'an. In fact, even reports from the *tābiʻūn* (followers of the companions) were examined and graded accordingly, either in *tafsīr* or *tajwīd*. As Qur'anic exegesis became an independent science, it was called *tafsīr* by the scholars themselves, and extensive studies of the usage of the Qurayshi dialect (i.e. the dialect of the Prophet's clan) became imperative.

The non-Muslim (especially Jewish, Christian, and Greek) philosophical influences had to be dealt with too. This led scholars, as they did with the rules and regulations for the Hadith literature discussed above, to lay down separate conditions for all *mufassirūn* (the Quranic exegetes or experts). Imam Ibn Taymiyyah recounts the list of these rules as explained by Ahmad Von Denffer.[26] The *mufassirūn* generally must:

- be of sound belief and be a man of piety (*taqwah*)
- be well grounded in the knowledge of Arabic and its grammatical rules
- be knowledgeable in other sciences connected with the study of the Qur'an (history, sharī'ah, uṣūl al-fiqh, tajwīd, etc.)
- possess ability for proper understanding
- not use mere opinion in his interpretations
- always begin his *tafsīr* of the Qur'an by consulting other verses of the Qur'an
- possess sound knowledge
- always use the Hadith in conjunction with the Qur'an
- always seek the companions' opinions after consulting the Hadith
- consider the *tābi'ūn's* interpretation next to the *ṣaḥābah's*
- consult other reputable scholars' opinions.

All of the above were not pointers intended to unify all *mufassirūns'* opinions in their *tafsīr* books. Instead, these early scholars achieved unity with the majority of the scholars of the various Muslim factions to follow the basic rules before extending their explanations to include whichever aspects of human life they intended to explore. Therefore, the only achievable aim was for the early scholars to lay down these guidelines, as the Qur'an is so vast in its meanings that no scholar can be well grounded in all ramifications of the entire knowledge contained therein:

> From eschatology and metaphysics to prayer and worship, from epistemology to individual conduct and social behaviour, from social philosophy to the problem of familial and societal organization, from theology to law and morality, from the most sensitive aspect of motivation to the explicit problems of war and peace, to justice and *Ihsan*, to history and futurology.[27]

All early Muslim factions agreed with the above rules of *tafsīr* except the Shīʿa, who disagreed with the last four conditions. The Shīʿi Hadith, meant to buttress their interpretations of the Qur'an, are separately compiled and are thus different from the general Sunni collections. Also, the Shī ʿa see no need to rely on the verdicts of the companions because the Shīʿa view the companions as being no better than all other Muslims. Instead, the Shīʿi imams' opinions completely overrule and supersede those of the *ṣaḥābah*, let alone any *tābiʿūn's*. The opinions to be consulted are those of the Shīʿi scholars.

Most of the early *tafsīr* books followed the general rules stated above. But unfortunately, few of those books survived. The only of this kind to survive until today comes from an outstanding scholar of the time, Muhammad ibn Jarīr al-Ṭabari (d.923 CE), who quotes the Hadith in full and provides a comprehensive *isnād* list to explain and interpret the Qur'an before arriving at his own opinion. *Tafsīr* books by ʿAbdullāh ibn ʿAbbās (a companion) also exist, but these were compiled later by another scholar, Muhammad b. Yaʿqūb al-Fayrūzābādī (d.1414 CE).) 'In any sense,' says Watt, 'this work of al-Ṭabari marks the close of an era, and prepares the way for the opening of another.'[28]

Tajwīd (Qur'an Recitation)

Tajwīd is the correct oral rendering of the Qur'an, preserving the nature of revelation and guarding it from distortion by using a comprehensive set of regulations to govern many of the parameters of sound production.[29] In other words, *tajwīd* is 'the codification of the sound of revelation as it was revealed to the Prophet Muhammad, and as he subsequently rehearsed it with the Angel Gabriel.'[30]

Although the Qur'an was revealed to the Prophet in his own Qurayshi dialect, the Qur'an was, according to him, also recited to him by the angel Jibrīl in seven different dialects, including Qurayshi. The Prophet allowed his followers to recite the Qur'an in any of those seven Arab dialects. This was probably because he took into account human nature, as people of the same tribe, speaking the same language, at times find it difficult to pronounce words outside their own dialect. In fact, this is a common phenomenon across the world today.

Based on the Prophet's approval, many learned *ṣaḥābah*,[31] in addition to having memorised the Qur'an, had their personal Qur'an written in various dialects. According to Abu Ameenah Bilal Philips, 'In some cases, each tribe used different words to describe the same object. For example, some tribes called the lion an *asad* while others called it a *layt*, *hamzah*, *hafs*, or a *ghadanfar*.'[32] In some cases, the same letters were pronounced differently.

After the Prophet died, Abu Bakr commissioned Zaid ibn Thābit to compile the Qur'an as a single book (from various inscribed sources like parchments, pieces of leather, slabs of bone, or stones). This compilation still contained dialectical variations because the whole Qur'an written in front of the Prophet was written by various scribes belonging to different Arab tribes.

'Uthmān, during his caliphate, commissioned four of the most learned *ṣaḥābah*[33] in Qur'anic recitation to produce seven copies of the Qur'an only in the Prophet's (Qurayshi) dialect. This was because dispute had arisen concerning the correct mode of recitation regarding the various dialects.[34]

Despite the fact that the four-member committee consisted of people who had memorised the entire Qur'an, they invited all people from all of the provinces who had memorised the Qur'an to be present each day throughout the period of the assignment to authenticate what was written by comparing it with what each memoriser had memorised directly from the Prophet. Six of the seven resulting copies of the Qur'an were sent to Makkah, Syria, Basra, Kufa, Yemen, and Bahrain, with one remaining with Caliph 'Uthmān in Madīnah.[35] Thus, with this restriction of using only material recited in the Qurayshi dialect, all other versions of the Qur'an were destroyed once all the memorisers had ratified the seven copies, testifying that they recounted the true revelations to the Prophet.

It cannot be stated with certainty that all those who possessed unapproved copies of the Qur'an immediately destroyed them. Indeed, some retained a few portions of these copies for some time. For instance, Imam Mālik used to show few pages of the Qur'an copied by his grandfather to some of his students. Some examples of the variant readings therein include the following, as noted by Yasin Dutton, a professor of Arabic:[36]

- *wa-awṣā* instead of *wa-waṣṣā* (*al-Baqarah* 2:132)
- *man yartadid* instead of *man yartadda* (*al-Mā'idah* 5:54)
- *alladhīna* instead of *wa-lladhīna* (*al-Tawbah* 9:107)
- *fa-tawakkal* instead of *wa-tawakkal* (*al-Shuʿarā'* 26:217)
- *mā tashtahī* instead of *mā tashtahīhi* (*al-Zukhruf* 43:71)
- *fa-lā yakhāfu* instead of *wa-lā yakhāfu* (*al-Shams* 91:15).

Another problem arose when Islam spread to non-Arab regions. The existing copies of the Qur'an had been written without any provisions for non-Arabs to read the Arabic, such that no vowels existed to supplement the consonants for proper pronunciation. That is, the Arabic was written 'without dashes (*tashkeel*, i.e. *fat-ḥah*, *kasrah* and *dammah*) to indicate the vowels, and without dots (*nuqāt*) to distinguish between look-alike letters (e.g. *seen* and *sheen*, ṣaad and ḍaad). The verses were not numbered, nor were there any punctuation signs to indicate pause or even the ending of verses'.[37]

To solve this problem, the governor of Basra at the time, Ziyād, commissioned one of the best grammarians of the time, Abu al-Aswad al-Du'ali (d.638 CE), to take up the assignment. At first, a dot (.) above a letter meant *fat-ḥah*, with the dot below the beginning of a letter being a *kasra*, and with the dot at the end of a letter being a dammah. All of these were later changed to a straight line (ـَ), above being *fat-ḥah*, and below being *kasrah*, and with a small *waw* above being a dammah.[38] All along, the originality of the Qur'an was perfectly maintained, as every generation up to today had its numerous memorisers of the Qur'an in all Muslim-dominated localities.

However, even with the unification of the 'Uthmān edition based on the Qurayshi dialect and the destruction of all other editions, a few learned companions teaching the Qur'an in various centres read the Qur'an in various dialects (in addition to Qurayshi). They explained to their students that though the official reading was in Qurayshi, the Prophet also allowed them to pronounce certain words differently in certain other dialects. Therefore, the transmission of unofficial recitations of the Qur'an continued during every generation, until Qur'an recitation later became an autonomous science.

It should be affirmed here that similar problems confronting the Hadith literature slightly affected the modes of Qur'anic recitation, as additional modes of unofficial recitation had already crept in, though these showed no forgeries as with the Hadith, seeing that these recitations did not change Qur'anic wording or meanings. These came about through the attempts of some scholars to make their recitations sound more melodious than the other scholars. By the middle of the tenth century CE, the number of unofficial recitations was as many as fourteen.

Scholars/reciters of the Qur'an tackled this problem by using methods similar to those used when dealing with the Hadith literature. Hence, conditions were laid down for the acceptance or rejection of any of the fourteen modes of recitation being propagated by different outstanding reciters. To condemn a single mode without providing convincing Islamic reasons would definitely add to the existing *fitnah*. Thus, the following conditions were laid down:

- Firstly, the mode of recitation must be traceable to the Prophet with authentic, unbroken chains of transmission or narration, and with discernible chains of transmission throughout the generations between the transmitters and the Prophet.
- Secondly, however sound and beautiful the recitation may be, it must not contradict the already established Arabic grammar, because there is not a single grammatical error in the Holy Qur'an.
- Thirdly, the recitation must agree with the official 'Uthmān edition, with only minor variations in pronunciation allowed.

This means that substituting alternative words or synonyms for the official Qurayshi ones was no longer allowed.

With all the above efforts, scholars were able to establish the seven approved modes of recitation. The recitations championed by the following outstanding scholars were selected (as compiled by Ahmad Von Denffer):[39]

Place	*Reciter*	*Transmitter*
1. Kufa	ʿĀṣim	Ḥafṣ
2. Kufa	Hamzah	
3. Kufa	al-Kisāʾī	Dūrī
4. Madīnah	Nāfiʿ	Warsh
5. Makkah	Ibn Kathīr	
6. Damascus	Ibn ʿĀmir	
7. Basra	Abu ʿĀmir	

The following seven were not rated like the above, but they were not condemned:

Place	*Reciter*
8. Madīnah	Abu Jaʿfar
9. Basra	Yaʿqūb
10. Basra	Hasan al-Baṣri
11. Basra	Yaḥya al-Yazīdī
12. Kufa	Khalaf
13. Kufa	al-Aʿmash
14. Makkah	Ibn Muḥayṣin

Therefore, starting from the tenth century CE, scholars have united Muslims of whatever factions on the seven modes of recitation and have saved the Qur'an from further proliferation of recitations. Out of the seven rated recitations, number one, transmitted by Ḥafs, is the most popular throughout the world, while number four, transmitted by Warsh, is popular throughout Africa (except Egypt).[40]

It helps us better appreciate the effort of the past scholars when we know that despite the written processes the Qur'an has undergone, there is no difference between the contemporary printed Qur'an and the original versions produced by the *ṣaḥābah* under Caliph 'Uthmān except the modes of writing (explained earlier) to simplify its recitation.

Out of 'Uthmān's seven versions (i.e. the original writings of the Prophet's companions), two remain intact today. One exists in Tashkent (Uzbekistan), and the other is in Columbia University's library.[41] Anyone may compare these with the contemporary printed copies of the Holy Qur'an. The recent discovery of some pages of the original copies in July 2015 at the University of Birmingham, United Kingdom, is an additional thrilling confirmation of the Qur'an's authenticity, as the pages contain the exact text as the present version. 'The message was clear,' says the University, 'by holding a fragment of the Qur'an dated to a period correlating closely with the lifetime of the Prophet Muhammad, the University of Birmingham possessed within its collections both a genuine global treasure and a sacred document of immense significance.'[42]

Fiqh (Jurisprudence)

The Holy Qur'an and Hadith remain as the authoritative sources of Islamic law (sharī'ah). According to al-Shahrastāni, the texts (the Qur'an and the Sunnah) are limited explicitly in their general details, while the situations, daily occurrences, and life experiences they describe are unlimited. Hence, *ijtihād* and analogy must be considered so that every situation may be brought within the compass of sharī'ah.[43]

It was amid this background that *fiqh* and *uṣūl al-fiqh* were developed by scholars of an independent branch of Islamic science to cater for the necessary needs of Muslims of all generations. *Fiqh*, as defined by the professor of Islamic law Mohammed Hisham Kamali, concerns itself with the knowledge of the detailed rules of Islamic law (sharī'ah) and its various branches. *Uṣūl* is all about the methods applied in the deduction of such rules from their sources. It means that '*fiqh* is the law itself where as *uṣūl al-fiqh* is the methodology of the law. The relationship between the two disciplines resembles that of the rules of grammar to the language or of logic (*manṭiq*) to Philosophy'.[44] In other words, *fiqh* is an extension of sharīʿah law as it applies to situations and occurrences that are not specifically or explicitly covered by both the Qur'an and the Sunnah.

Thus, with the above clear meanings, it is obvious that sharīʿah as a whole was already in existence during the Prophet's period. But after him, many of his companions migrated to various newly conquered regions and were faced with new situations and occurrences. Those who remained in Ḥijāz (Makkah and Madīnah) faced lesser challenges because most of the laws accounted for their (Arab) cultural heritage. They had enough Qur'an- and Hadith-based texts to buttress their verdicts. Besides, the administration of the first three caliphs was centred in Ḥijāz. These caliphs had modified some laws, and through the consensus of other *ṣaḥābah* or by way of the caliphs' independent opinions (*ra'y*), they solved many cases which might be faced by the early Arab Muslims. This assisted the companions who settled either in Makkah (e.g. 'Abdullāh b. 'Abbās) or Madīnah (e.g. 'Abdullāh b. 'Umar), leading them to rely mostly on the texts.

'There were other *ṣaḥābah* who favoured the wide use of personal opinions [*ra'y*] in areas undefined by the Qur'ān or Sunnah.'[45] 'Abdullāh b. Masʿūd was among the leading companions in the use of *ra'y*. He settled in Iraq, where various new converts from different races and cultural heritages resided. The use of *ra'y* was, therefore, more frequent in the new centres like Basra and Kufa in Iraq.

The students of these companions (the *tābiʿūn*) followed the legacies of their teachers (the companions) in different regions. That is why, for instance, Abu Ḥanīfah's use of reasoning 'was in fact the common method used by the Iraqi jurists'.[46] The reason for Imam Mālik's strict adherence to the Hadith was that he honoured the legacy of the companions in

Ḥijāz. This does not mean that the Ḥijāzi scholars did not use *ra'y* at all. They used it when it was absolutely necessary, such as when no single verse or Hadith was available to give judgement.[47]

The Ḥijāzi scholars did not bother themselves with speculative or hypothetical situations. However, the Iraqi scholars were faced with different cultural challenges, such as Greek philosophical questions and non-Muslim (Jewish, Christian, and freethinking) ideologies. So, scholars in Iraq unavoidably had to tackle speculative and hypothetical questions which the Prophet and the Rightly Guided Caliphs, especially the first three, had not answered.[48]

Each centre of learning produced many scholars who gave their *fatwas*, or verdicts, to their followers according to their understanding of the Qur'an, the availability of Hadiths in their possession, and the legacies of the previous pious *ṣaḥābah*. The problem of sectarian divisions was already a huge challenge, but now it was coupled with rivalry between individual scholars, even in a single city. This had started during the Umayyad caliphates and continued to the Abbasid era, when judges were appointed from among the favoured scholars and had unrestricted power, no unifying influence from central government, and no hierarchy (including superior courts) to set binding precedents.[49] Instead, the court organised debates among these scholars, and whoever won usually earned a monetary reward and prestige. Each founder of a *madh-hab* (i.e. a school of jurisprudence) had to protect his honour and school at all costs, 'because loss of personal prestige also entailed loss of prestige on the part of one's *madh-hab*, the principle of defending one's madhhab, right or wrong came to be considered a virtue'.[50]

The rulers and the wealthy who were the sponsors of institutions of learning restricted themselves and their subjects to their favourite *madhhabs*, not allowing Muslims to benefit much from equally competent scholars. As a result, other scholars and their followers felt offended. This added to the existing hatred and division. In the resulting battle for survival, the followers of these scholars became staunch enemies, condemning one another freely.

According to the venerated *fiqh* scholar Sayyid Sābiq, equally competent scholars were not favoured with appointment to political office like the jurists of the four madhhabs were. 'They are not allowed to become judges, and people are discouraged from following their rulings by accusing them of innovations.'[51] According to Abu Zahra, 'The level of disagreement became intense and impassioned. [The scholars] were severe with one another and started to accuse one another of disbelief, inequality and rebellion.'[52] In his *Fiqh al-Sunnah*, Sābiq affirms that despite the fact that these scholars, especially the four imams, forbade people from following them blindly, 'the people after them exaggerated their importance and began to follow them more and more blindly. Every group thought it sufficient just to follow what was found in their school of thought.' He continues:

> Blind observance of one madhhab caused the Muslim nation to lose the guidance of the Qur'an and sunnah. The door of juristic reasoning was closed. The Shari'ah became the statement of the jurists, and the statement of jurists became the Shari'ah. Anyone who differed from what they said was regarded as an innovator, whose words were neither to be trusted nor followed.
>
> As a result, the Muslim nation broke into different groups and sects to such an extent that they differed over whether or not it was permissible for a follower of the Hanafi madhhab to marry a woman of the Shafi'i *madhhab*. Some said that such marriage would not be valid because the Shafi'i woman's faith was in doubt. Others said that such marriage is valid by analogy to marriage with the people of the book.[53]

No doubt, the four imams were outstanding scholars in knowledge, morality, and religiosity. Few other scholars possessed these qualities, unfortunately their schools lacked political backing. Furthermore, some tough arguments and condemnations centred on the scholars' application of *uṣūl al-fiqh*. Of course, the jurists (*fuqahāh*) believed in the Qur'an, the Sunnah, *ijmā'* (agreement of opinions on a particular issue), and *qiyās/ra'y* (an individual scholar's opinion derived from the three previous sources), but their application of other sources apart from the Qur'an and the Sunnah, chronologically in order of importance, differed from one scholar to the other. This was part of the reasons for their accusations against and condemnations of one another.

It is noteworthy that at this time these scholars relied on the limited Hadith that was available to individuals in their city or region. For instance, Imam Mālik made all of his judgements based on the Qur'an and Hadith collected only in Madīnah. When asked by Caliph Harūn al-Rashīd why there were no Hadiths reported by 'Ali and Ibn 'Abbās in his *al-Muwaṭṭa'*, Imam Mālik said, 'They were not in my home town and I did not meet their transmitters.'[54]

Although all the Hadiths in *al-Muwaṭṭa'* are authentic, this buttresses the fact that some other scholars had consulted unreliable Hadiths in reaching their verdicts, as Hadith codification (discussed earlier) had not yet taken place.[55] These scholars had not applied those strict rules to the Hadith by which many of their collections have been shown not to meet the set standard. This was why, at the time, some jurists renounced their long-held opinions and verdicts when faced with more authentic Hadiths than those which they previously consulted. A few of these scholars were caught up in one sectarian division or the other, giving their *fatwas* according to their doctrinal opinions.

In addition, 'lies about the Prophet proliferated in this period because various groups defended their positions unscrupulously with words which led to the spread of forged Ḥadīth'.[56] This added to the Iraqi scholars' decision to meticulously restrict the use of Hadith. These were some of the challenges faced by *fiqh* and the *fuqahāh*.

The above issues point out the extent of the division which had existed in the past among the jurists; the negative impact of political leaders on scholars and Muslims; and some specific scholars' rigid arrogation of knowledge, and unwillingness to listen to or even consider other scholars' views, verdicts, or opinions. All of these things are hindrances to unity, tolerance, broad-mindedness, and the internal security of Muslims, past and present.

When the Abbasid took over from the Umayyad, the early Abbasid caliphs patronised and respected the Islamic scholars. This was because the caliphs claimed that they wanted to restore a Sharī'ah base to the caliphate. Therefore, Islamic scholarship flourished. The caliphs sent their children to various scholars to learn, and a few of them even joined the ranks of the scholars, like Caliph Harūn al-Rashīd (786–809 CE).[57] At this time in history, individual scholars' *fatwas* and their schools of thought were attached to their names (as the *madh-hab* of so-and-so), with their various styles of *uṣūl* and their methodology for applying Sharī'ah or *fiqh*.

At the beginning of the Abbasid, 'Ibn al-Muqaffa' urged Caliph al-Manṣūr to work for agreement on legal principles between the various ancient schools; and this may have had a slight effect' on unifying the various sects of Muslims.[58] This unresolved disagreement prompted Imam al-Shāfi'i to take up the challenge. 'Disputation and diversity of juristic thought in different quarters accentuated the need for clear guidance, and the time was ripe for al-Shāfi'i to articulate the methodology of *uṣūl al-fiqh*.'[59]

Imam al-Shāfi'i came on the scene at a time of conflict and condemnation between the jurists of Ḥijāz and Iraq known as *Ahl al-Hadith* and *Ahl al-Ra'y* respectively. Of course, *uṣūl al-fiqh* was in existence before al-Shāfi'i, but no one had comprehensively systematised it like he had. Not only did Imam al-Shāfi'i freely discourage the use of things like customs (of the past scholars) and personal opinions (of the present scholars), but also he redefined the method of legal reasoning and restricted it to the framework of the authoritative sources.[60]

All reputable jurists unanimously agreed that the Hadith was second only to the Qur'an, but they differed among themselves on the reliability of certain Hadiths, especially those reported by only one person. For instance, Imam Abu Ḥanīfah and Imam Mālik did not consider such Hadiths as being superior to *qiyās*. Imam Mālik preferred *qiyās* to such Hadiths, reported by only one person, which were not supported by the practices of the companions and/or the *tābi'ūn*. Imam Abu

Ḥanīfah accepted some of them and rejected others based on his own strict scrutiny. He accepted them in dealing with ordinary matters if he was satisfied about the instinct of the reporter, but in dealing with intricate legal matters, he rejected them unless they were supported by circumstantial evidence and fundamental Islamic principles.[61]

Imam al-Shāfi'i devotes Chapter 5 of his book *al-Risālah* to 'the obligation of man to accept the authority of the Prophet'. In many of his other books, he tries to convince people of this by citing numerous Hadiths in which the Prophet accepted reports from only one of his companions, saying that the companions did the same. Not only this, but Imam al-Shāfi'i even says that the texts of the Hadiths which are not in contradiction with any Qur'anic verses but for which no text of the Qur'an is plainly found to confirm them should also be accepted. He writes in *al-Risālah*, 'As for the Sunnah which he [the Prophet] laid down on matters for which a text is not found in the Book of God, the obligation to accept them rests upon us by virtue of the duty imposed by God to obey [the Prophet's] orders.'[62]

The contribution of al-Shāfi'i in this regard is meant to solve the problem of conflict between and condemnation of one another through the scholars' different rankings of *ra'y*, or companion and *tābi'ūn* opinions, as being against some doubtful Hadiths, especially those reported by only one person. He does this by securing a dominant status for the Sunnah and proving that '*al-sunnah qādiyan 'ala al-Qur'ān*, that is, the Sunnah is the decisive authority for determining the meaning of the text of the Qur'ān'.[63] The efforts of Imam al-Shāfi'i initially added to the conflicts, as he was seen as a critic of his teacher, Imam Mālik, and of other jurists.

However, thanks to the efforts of Hadith specialists and their criticisms, codifications, and final ranking or grading of all the traditions, the use of individual localised Hadiths by various *fuqahāh* became part of history. The Hadith of the Prophet, in whatever corner of the Islamic world, were codified into accessible collections, were certified, and were ratified by specialists trusted by Muslims. This, therefore, buttressed the efforts of al-Shāfiʿi to secure a dominant status for the Sunnah. In addition to ranking the Qur'an and Hadith (whether reported by numerous companions or only one companion), individual scholars could rank other branches of *uṣūl al-fiqh* according to their school of thought.

The negative side of politically backing only a few scholars is mentioned above, but the restriction is not without its advantages, as the proliferation of numerous *madh-habs* would lead to too many conflicting opinions to cope with, especially by the imams' followers. Today, only four of these imams are regarded as authorities across the Sunni world: Imams Abu Ḥanīfah, Mālik, al-Shāfiʿi, and Ibn Ḥanbal.[64]

'The four schools, then, are equally covered by Ijmā'. They are all deemed to translate into individual legal rules the will of Allah as expressed in the Kor'an and in the Sunna of the Prophet; their alternative interpretations are all equally valid, their methods of reasoning equally legitimate; in short, they are equally orthodox.'[65]

All factions today, as numerous as they are, follow these imams, except the Shīʿa, who established their school of jurisprudence based on Shiʿism. The Muʿtazilah (another early sect) also tried to do the same but was excommunicated.

Section 2
Codification of Doctrines

Islamic scholars also looked into the codification of the various doctrinal beliefs of the existing numerous sects and factions of Islam. They accepted many and rejected others based on their strict assessment of which ones were wrong and which ones were right. They also unanimously agreed on some doctrines. The following beliefs are some of the major considerations.

Rejection of Createdness of the Holy Qur'an

The Mu'tazilah was among the most popular and most influential sects in the early period of Islam. This sect invented the doctrine of the createdness of the Holy Qur'an. That is, they claimed that the Qur'an is a creature like all beings. They said that if the Qur'an is not believed to be created, then this throws the absolute unity of Allah into question. Contrarily, other scholars believed that the Holy Book, as the words of Allah that emanated directly from the knowledge of Allah, is definitely eternal and uncreated. That is, any knowledge emanating from Allah is divine and not created, as Allah, the author of the holy words, is uncreated. These contradictory beliefs about the Qur'an led to many conflicts, much hatred, and numerous revolts.

During the caliphate of al-Ma'mūn (198 AH–218 AH/813–833 CE), the caliph was attracted to some Mu'tazili doctrines, especially that of the createdness of the Holy Qur'an. He therefore appointed Mu'tazilites to various political offices. This boosted the popularity of this sect and the official recognition of its doctrines. In 212 AH/827 CE, al-Ma'mūn officially declared his belief in the Mu'tazili doctrine of the createdness of the Qur'an. A few months prior to his death, he officially issued a *miḥna* (an inquisition or ordeal to test a Muslim's faith) in order to identify those who refused to believe in the Mu'tazili concept of the createdness of the Qur'an. He sent this to all provincial governors and judges (*qāḍīs*) to test them first and then to have them enforce the law in their respective domains.

This increased the existing hatred and division, as those who refused to recognise the *miḥna* were persecuted. Some were imprisoned, whereas others were tortured to death. According to Professor Matroudi, only those who believed in the createdness of the Qur'an were to hold government positions. In fact, testimony in court was accepted only from those who believed in this *miḥna*. An inquisition was established to interrogate scholars so as to discover those who supported the *miḥna* and those who did not, and to punish whoever refused to support it.[66] As respected as Imam Aḥmad b. Ḥanbal was, he was tortured and imprisoned for his refusal to recognise the inquisition.

Al-Ma'mūn died shortly after he issued the *miḥna*, and Imam Aḥmad b. Ḥanbal was subsequently released from prison. Two of the successive caliphs, al-Mu'tasim and al-Wāthiq, continued to enforce the law. In fact, there was a popular revolt against the *miḥna* under al-Wāthiq in Baghdad. An eminent Hadith scholar, Aḥmad ibn Naṣr al-Khuzā'i, led the revolt. It was an unsuccessful revolt, as Ibn Naṣr was arrested and executed in Sha'bān in 231 AH/April 846 CE.[67]

Al-Mutawakkil succeeded his brother al-Wāthiq in 232 AH/847 CE and changed the course of events. The new caliph demonstrated his lack of interest in the *miḥna*. First, he stopped the persecution of people, and then he prohibited the doctrine of the createdness of the Qur'an. He also encouraged Islamic scholars to refute the dogma of the Mu'tazilites.[68] Although al-Mutawakkil was assassinated around 247 AH/861 CE, Islamic scholars continued the struggle to ensure that Mu'tazilism remained prohibited[69] and that the majority's belief in the uncreatedness of the Qur'an was firmly established. In addition, the Muʿtazilites were not incorporated into the mainstream *Ahl al-Sunnah* community. They were excommunicated.

Status of the Caliphs and the Ṣaḥābah

One of the most serious hindrances to the unity and conciliation of the early Muslims was the ranking of the four Rightly Guided Caliphs above the others, including their acceptance in order of their chronology, along with the declaration of all *ṣaḥābah* (companions) as being equally righteous without exception. The conflicting rating of the caliphs, especially Caliph ʿUthmān and Caliph ʿAli, troubled political leaders, Islamic scholars, and members of the various Muslim factions.

The political doctrine of the Murjiʿah (one of the early sects) states that Murjiʿites should be neutral in the rating of a particular caliph above the others, especially as concerned ʿUthmān and ʿAli, as each caliph was preferred by a certain group of people and not by others. Abu Bakr was accepted by many Muslims but was rejected by the Shīʿa. ʿUmar was rated highest by the Khārijites, ʿUthmān was the most beloved of the Umayyad and their supporters, while ʿAli was considered by the Shīʿa to be the best.

Trying to reconcile this issue was so tough that it even engulfed the four outstanding founders of Sunni schools of jurisprudence. One of the ʿAlawites asked Imam Mālik, 'Who are the best of people after the Prophet?' Imam Mālik mentioned Abu Bakr, ʿUmar, and ʿUthmān chronologically, and then stopped. When questioned why he did not mention ʿAli, he said, 'Some one who seeks leadership is not equal to some one who does not seek it.' He rated ʿAli as one of the most honoured companions.[70] Imam Ibn Ḥanbal affirmed the first three caliphs (Abu Bakr, ʿUmar, and ʿUthmān) as the best after the Prophet. Next to them were the shūra members[71] [ʿAli, Saʿd, Ṭalḥah, Zubair, and ʿAbd-al-Raḥmān]. To him, ʿAli was rated above other companions but was not of the same status as the other caliphs. As for al-Shāfiʿi, he affirmed the four but proclaimed his love for 'Ali, which made his opponents suspect him of being a Shī'a.[72] Imam Abu Ḥanīfah, believed to be a Murji'ite, upheld the four as the true caliphs (with the status of being next to the Prophet). He proclaims in *al-Fiqh al-Akbar*, article 5, 'We leave the question of 'Uthmān and 'Ali to God.'[73]

Probably on account of the misdeeds of the Umayyad during Caliph 'Uthmān's reign, some Muslims preferred to rate 'Ali above 'Uthmān. In fact, Caliph al-Ma'mūn officially declared 'Ali above 'Uthmān, whereas the Mu'tazilites had divided opinions. The Basran Mu'tazilites rated 'Uthmān as number three, while their counterparts in Baghdad rated 'Ali above 'Uthmān. This confusion and conflict remained until the ninth or tenth century, and then a bold decision was taken.

> To make 'Ali third was a partial rejection of 'Uthman, and this was intolerable to many among the main body of Muslims. By the later ninth century it had become clear that for the main body of Muslims to remain united the only satisfactory identity was an identity with the whole past history of Islam (or at least the whole of its early history) and that this implied the acceptance of 'Uthman as best qualified to the rules at the time he became Caliph.[74]

Scholars of various factions, including the Ash'ariyyah and their supporters who participated in the articulation of Sunnism, agreed on their ratings based on the chronological order of the caliphs' elections. Imam al-Ghazzāli, amongst many other scholars, codifies this in his *Iḥyā' 'ulūm al-Dīn*.

The rightful imams, or leaders, after the Prophet are Abu Bakr, then 'Umar, then 'Uthmān, and then 'Ali. The Prophet's attention was not upon any particular leader.[75] This was the agreement of all Muslims except the Shī'a, who rejected the first three caliphs and believed them to be usurpers of 'Ali's right. In order to be accepted as a member of the Sunni community, al-Ghazzāli, in addition to many others, says that one must believe in the chronological order of these caliphs based on their respective election to the caliphate.[76]

Against the belief of the Shīʿa in a hidden imam or leader, the Sunnis unanimously agreed that any Muslim leader must be present, not be hidden to his subjects, not be awaited, and not necessarily be infallible or the best in the community so long as he can maintain excellent justice and command the respect of his people.

Concerning the issue of election of these caliphs from a particular tribe or clan, almost all factions agreed that the election of a leader was a necessity. The Ashʿarites, Shiʿites, and Muʿtazilites, and most of the Khārijites, believed in the necessity of leadership, or imamate. This was also the agreement of the Sunni.[77] However, the disagreement was based upon whether or not the leader was the better qualified among the Qurayshi generally or specifically from the Prophet's clan or ʿAli's descendants, or among all qualified Muslims. The Shīʿa made it compulsory that ʿAli's descendants be only qualified persons from the Qurayshi family, while the Khārijites preferred a leader from any tribe or race, not necessarily an Arab. According to al-Ghazzāli, the following is required for a leader to be part of the Sunni community:

> It is to believe that a leader, in addition to his qualification of being a Muslim, mature and intelligent, must have five other qualities: must be a male, God fearing, learned, competent and be a Qurayshi tribe because the Prophet says: leaders are from the Quraysh. With all these qualities, such a man is qualified as a leader as long as he has the support of the majority. The minority who oppose such decision must be brought under control because they are termed as rebels.[78]

On the issue of the companions, scholars agreed that no distinction was to be made among them, as they were all sincere and righteous. Some Muslims, especially the Khārijites, condemned some companions like ʿAmr ibn al-ʿĀs, Muʿāwiyah and Abu Mūsā al-Ashʿari. In addition, Ṭalḥah, Zubair, ʿAli, and ʿĀishah were formerly regarded as sincere, but when conflicts broke out between them, they could no longer be trusted. The Muʿtazilites said that one party among them must be wrong and another party must be right; however, which one is wrong and which one is right is known only to Allah. As for the Shīʿa, they condemned most of the *ṣaḥābah*. Their reasons for this will be discussed in the next chapter. Sunni scholars, on the other hand, insisted that all companions were righteous. Imam Ibn Ḥanbal said that the condemned people were included in the general circle of the Prophet's companions described by Allah: 'their mark is on their faces, the traces of prostration' (*al-Fatḥ* 48:29).[79]

Caliph al-Mutawakkil assisted the scholars politically by trying to impose the death penalty on whoever insulted either the Prophet's wives specifically or the companions in general.

Other Theological Issues

Based on different scholars' understandings of the Qur'an and the Sunnah, the following are some theological agreements of the *Ahl al-Sunnah wa'l-Jamā'ah* as explained by al-Ash'arī, al-Ghazzāli, and al-Shahrastāni:

a) The Sunni scholars accepted and adopted the style of dialectic theology (*kalām*)[80] of al-Ash'ari and al-Maturīdī. This is because, as the Mu'tazilites became a separate sect with their *kalām*, the Ash'arites and Maturīdīs applied the *kalām* to buttress the beliefs, views, and doctrines of the Sunni majority.
b) Some Khārijites and Mu'tazilites denied questioning in the grave, but whoever was to be accepted into the Sunni fold must believe in questioning in the grave by the funerary angels Munkar and Nakīr. According to al-Shahrastāni, it is best to regard this questioning as being addressed neither to the disembodied spirit nor to the present body. If these angels question the dead about belief alone, the spirit (*rūḥ*) could answer; but if questions about one's beliefs, words, and deeds should come up, the body in its proper form would have to be assembled. If the state of a person in the grave is like that of a sleeper or drunkard, it is possible for God to quicken the organs of thought and speech to respond appropriately.[81]
c) In addition, every Sunni must believe in punishment in the grave, resurrection after death, the bridge to be crossed by everyone,

and the scale for measuring human deeds. Regarding the scale that weighs or measures a person's deeds, al-Shahrastāni says that it is best to prove 'that every terrestrial has a fitting scale; the scale of the ponderable is the ordinary scale of weight; the scale of dry weight is the gallon, of length is cubit and so on; and the scale of deeds is what God knows best as fitting for such'.[82] God has clearly declared that He will set up a balance/weight on the Day of Judgement (*al-Anbiyā'* 21:48).

d) On the issue of grave sinners, Khārijites excommunicated them forever from Islam, while Mu'tazilites said they were neither Muslims nor unbelievers. To the Sunni, any Muslim facing *qiblah* (i.e. the Muslim direction of prayer) must not be declared as a *kāfir* regardless of his grave sin, so long as the sin is not related to *shirk*. And so long as such a Muslim has not died in a state of *shirk*, he is still a Muslim, but a *mushrik* Muslim (a polytheist Muslim). If he repents sincerely before he dies, Allah says, 'o my servants who have transgressed against their souls! Despair not of the mercy of Allah: *for Allah forgives all sins*: for He is Oft-Forgiving, Most Merciful' (*al-Zumr*, 39:53). In addition, apart from the ten *ṣaḥābah* (Abu Bakr, 'Umar, 'Uthmān, 'Ali, Ṭalḥah, Zubayr, 'Abdul-Raḥmān, Sa'd, Sa'īd, and Abu 'Ubaydah) mentioned by the Prophet, no one should be declared as going to, or being in, Paradise or Hell.[83] This is because entry into Paradise or Hell is one of the prerogatives of Allah, who can do whatever He likes. Moreover, a single sin is considered by Allah as one, whereas one good deed is multiplied ten times (*al-An'ām* 6:160). This presupposes that the mercy of Allah is limitless and that God forgives whomever He likes and punishes whomever He wills, for He has power over all things (*al-Baqarah* 2:284).

e) Based on the above, the scholars agreed that Muslims can pray behind any competent imam, whether pious or dissolute. Supplications for any Muslim departed souls, pious or not, were also approved, so long as they were facing *qiblah* (i.e. observing *ṣalāt* when they were alive). Giving alms (*ṣadaqāt*) on behalf of these departed souls, whether righteous or grave sinners, were approved so long as the individuals died as Muslims.

f) The scholars were against the Mu'tazili doctrine, which denies the current existence of Paradise and Hell. The Mu'tazilites asked how the two could currently be in existence when they were not performing their primary functions. The Mu'tazilites believed that Paradise and Hell would be in existence on the Day of Judgement. However, the Sunni argued that whoever wanted to be considered as part of the majority must believe that Paradise and Hell are already in existence because Allah says, 'Vie in haste for the forgiveness of your Lord and a Paradise which is as vast as the heaven and the earth, prepared for God-fearing ones' (*Āl-Imrān* 3:127). If Paradise and Hell were not already in existence, God would not have described the vastness of both to his believers.

g) The scholars also agreed that all *Ahl al-Sunnah wa'l-Jamā'ah* should believe in visions in sleep as well as miracles (*karāmāt*) of the pious ones. In addition, they must believe that witchcraft, wizard, and sorcery are all real in this world, even though they are all infidelities (*kufr*).

Toleration, Conciliation, and Elimination

It has been mentioned that the existing sects of Islam's early period were so numerous that a list of them could result in a moderate-sized pamphlet. Despite this huge number, scholars took bold steps to unite the sects into a single community.

It is therefore obvious from all mentioned above that Sunnism is a conglomeration of doctrines of various sects considered to be on the right path and a codification of the former dissenting views, verdicts, and opinions of different outstanding scholars. This achievement was made possible through tolerance, conciliation, the absorption of those divergent theological opinions, and the elimination of the few opinions considered to be on the errant path. Most all of the sects that refused to believe in all the doctrines of Sunnism were gradually eliminated and became part of history.

Even with the Muʿtazilites' political backing, brilliancy in oration, and excellence in philosophical argumentation, they were excommunicated together with their affiliates, the Qadarites, by the joint efforts of the Sunni scholars and some political leaders. The only sect which rejected some of the aforementioned major Sunni doctrines and survived eradication or elimination is the Shīʿa.

Since around the tenth century, the Shīʿa have remained as the only surviving Muslim sect outside the Sunni community. This means that the Jabrites, some of whom transformed into Ashʿarites, Murjiʿites, and some factions of Khārijites – with numerous other sects – all came together, through tolerance and conciliation, as a single community. 'The Ibadiyyah are the sole surviving sectarian relative of the Khārijites: they exist today primarily in Oman, Algeria, Libya, Tunis and along the Swahili Coast.'[84]

Perhaps one of the greatest examples of the toleration and conciliation effort is the acceptance of the Sūfis, who had been previously condemned as heretics. Their acceptance was based on the condition that they not commit themselves to assertions clearly known to be heretical according to pure Islamic dogma.[85] Thus, out of Sūfism's numerous factions, the followers of the following persons were approved and absorbed into mainstream Islam: al-Muḥāsibi, Ḥamdūn al-Qassār, Abu Yazīd al-Bisṭāmi, al-Junayd, al-Nūri, Sahl al-Tustari, al-Ḥakīm al-Tirmidhī, al-Kharrās, Ibn al-Khafīf, and al-Ṣayyāri.[86]

It is pertinent to mention here that Sūfis were tolerated largely because of Imam al-Ghazzāli's weight of protest. Before al-Ghazzāli, Sūfis 'and their devoted disciples, far from the beaten track of orthodoxy, had fostered a silent and powerless opposition to rigid formation and dogmatism. Now from Ghazzāli's mouth the Muslims could hear the loud protest of a respected doctor of orthodoxy'.[87] According to Watt, the toleration of Sufism probably 'gave strong support to Sunnism in the process of establishing itself'.[88]

Whence Comes the Name Sunni?

The Prophet of Islam left all his followers with the name *muslimūn* (Muslims) or *mu'minūn* (believers). These names, Muslim and Mu'min, as mentioned by the Qur'an in various places, are to date the general names of Prophet Muḥammad's followers. However, less than thirty years after the Prophet died, the first group of Muslims broke away from the camp of the fourth caliph, 'Ali b. Abi Ṭālib, and later became known as Khawārij (Khārijites). Since that time, various Muslim sects followed suit, with adopted separate names or names given to them by their opponents. As mentioned earlier, the rate of division was so great at one point that it was confusing to identify a particular group as being part of the main body of Muslims without mentioning the specific sectarian (second) name, or at least the name of the school of thought (*madhhab*) to which an individual belonged.

It is obvious, therefore, that the conglomeration of various sectarian views or dogmas formed the Sunni doctrines, whereas the entire doctrines rests on the codification of the Hadiths, as discussed earlier, since the Holy Qur'an remains as an authoritative Book binding all factions (whether eliminated or existing) together. The only major sect that rejected the general Hadith codification and survived elimination is the Shī'a.

This means that, whatever the *fiqh* of any faction, the Hadiths to buttress the verdicts rest on the codification of those rated and/or on some of the unrated ones. Whatever *tafsīr* any one person subscribes to, whatever modes of Qur'anic recitation, whatever preaching, new verdicts, new ideologies, or new lifestyle of any faction since that time, all rest on these same Hadith collections. This means that the articulation of Sunni Islam largely rests on the Hadith collections previously discussed. According to Professor of Islamic Studies Scott C. Lucas, 'The major ḥadith scholars of the third/ninth century played a far greater role in the articulation of Sunni Islam ... the Saḥīḥs of al-Bukhari and Muslim have remained the most exalted books, after the Qur'an, in the opinions of virtually all Sunni scholars of the past twelve centuries, a feast unmatched by any legal or theological work.'[89]

It was because of these reasons that Muslims of divergent views who came together then as a single community began to proudly associate themselves with the codification of such Hadiths as either *Ahl-al-Sunnah* or *Ahl-al-Ḥadīth*, as there was no such names recorded for any faction before the codification. Whereas the Shīʿa were proud to follow only the legacies of the *Ahl al-Bayt* (the family of the Prophet narrowed down to the chosen descendant imams of ʿAli and Fāṭimah), the Sunni majority felt that so long as they had codified the legacies of the entire life of the Prophet through his family and companions, their own identity would be 'the people of Sunnah generally' i.e. *Ahl al-Sunnah* of the Prophet, his family (wives and descendants) and his companions. The Sunni believed that only through these categories of people that Muslims could comprehensively understand the entire Islam.

According to Watt,[90] the common name for Sunni in later times was *Ahl al-Sunnat wa-l-Jamāʿa*, as mentioned by Abu al-Layth al-Samarqand (d.983). In *Sharḥ al-Fiqh al-Akbar*, Imam Aḥmad also mentioned *Ahl-al-Sunnat wa-l-Jamāʿa wa-l-Athar*. Ibn Qutayba (d.889) did likewise.[91] Al-Ashʿari (d.935), in his *Maqālāt al-Islāmiyyīn*, mentions in various places *Ahl-al-Sunnat wa-l-Istiqāmah*, especially when discussing the death of Caliph ʿUthmān as an unjust killing.[92] He also mentions *Aṣ-ḥāb al-Ḥadīth* when listing various early sects.[93] All these terms refer to the same faction. Similar terms had probably been mentioned by early scholars before al-Ashʿari, but definitely not before the codification of Hadith collections.

The inclusion of the term *Jamāʿah* with *Ahl-al-Sunnah* shows the Sunni's pride of being the Muslim majority, as opposed to the Shiʿite minority who rejected the popular Sunnah or Hadith collections approved by the majority. Still, even today, the Shīʿa make use of any Sunni Hadith which buttresses any of their doctrines, regardless of whichever of the Sunni records, either graded or not.

With the passage of time, the various terms mentioned above were shortened to simply 'Sunni', that is the followers, party, or people of Sunnah, or the short meaning of *Ahl al-Sunnah* (i.e. the party or people who stood in the practice of the codified Prophet's traditions or legacies through his wives, descendants and companions). According to Watt, the first mention of the adjective *Sunni* was made by Ibn-Baṭṭa (d.997). Today, whatever faction any Muslim identifies with, he or she belongs either to the Sunni majority or the Shiʿite minority, even though numerous sects abound within the two major dominant Muslim factions.

> It must be hailed as a great achievement that the Muslims were ready to accept certain differences within a common framework, first of all perhaps the seven *aḥruf* or *qirāʾāt*, and later the legal schools. This convergence, together with the acceptance of limited variation and the gradual elimination of deviant sects, must be ascribed in part to the strong feeling for the unity of the community found in many Muslims. This feeling probably indicated by the use of the word *jamāʿa* in the name Ahl-as-Sunna wa-l-Jamāʿa. It is perhaps also possible to trace the source of the feeling to a belief that the Islamic community is a charismatic community.[94]

Chapter 2

The Shī'a

Historical Background

'Hated by the Kharijites, resisted by the Syrians and Mu'āwiya's party, unloved by the Hijāzī supporters of Zubair, abandoned by the neutrals, and not well supported even by the Kufans … nonetheless, 'Ali still had zealous personal party.'[1] This is the summary of the pathetic circumstances surrounding 'Ali ibn Abi Ṭālib, which brought about the various misfortunes that befell him and his descendants and which also brought into existence the second faction of contemporary Muslims known as the Shī'a.

This name Shī'a is short for 'Shī'at 'Ali', meaning 'Ali's faction or party. Al-Shahrastāni, as quoted by William Montgomery Watt, describes Shi'ites as 'those who follow (*shāya'v̄*) 'Ali peace be on him in particular, and assert his imamate and caliphate by appointment and delegations (*naṣṣ*, *waṣiyya*) made either openly or secretly, and who believe that the imamate does not depart from his descendants'.[2] According to the Shi'ites, the Shī'a are a group of Muslims who, during the lifetime of the Prophet of God and after his death, regarded 'Ali as the rightful imam and caliph, and broke away from others and attached themselves to him.[3]

According to a Shi'ite scholar Ja'far Sobhani, the Prophet throughout his life emphasised the virtues, nobility, and leadership qualities of 'Ali. Based on this, some companions during the Prophet's lifetime formed a group around 'Ali known as Shī'a 'Ali (the followers of 'Ali), and these people were loyal to 'Ali throughout.[4] 'In this sense,' says Shi'ite scholar Arzina R. Lalani, 'Shi'ism is believed to have existed at the time of the Prophet, when a group of individuals including Salmān al-Fārisi, Abu Dhārr al-Ghiffāri, al-Miqdād b. al-Aswad al-Kindi and 'Ammār b. Yāsir used to be referred to as Shī'at 'Ali and Aṣḥāb 'Ali.'[5]

Immediately after the death of the Prophet Muḥammad (pbuh), Muslims divided themselves into three main factions: the Anṣār, who wanted to make a Madīnan the leader; the Muhājirūn and part of the Anṣār, who wanted to do likewise from the Qurayshi family; and the third party, Banū Hāshim, and few friends of 'Ali, who favoured 'Ali. Abu Bakr was finally elected from the Quraysh.

The confusion over who was to be elected after the Prophet died was the result of the fact that most of the sayings, actions, and attitudes of the Prophet indicated that he favoured both Abu Bakr and 'Ali. Some Muslims expected 'Ali b. Abi Ṭālib to be elected after Abu Bakr since both of them were the Prophet's candidates. But alas, 'Umar al-Khaṭṭāb was selected by Abu Bakr to be the next leader after him.

After the death of the second caliph, 'Umar, instead of the second candidate of the Prophet, 'Ali, being elected, another eminent companion, 'Uthmān, was enthroned by the six-member council comprised of the most respected companions, including 'Ali himself. There was no problem in the first half (six years) of 'Uthmān's reign. But in the second half (another six years), problems of various kinds (tribalism, nepotism, and some forms of corruption) engulfed the caliphate of 'Uthmān. According to a Shi'ite scholar, Syed Amir Ali:

> The personality of 'Uthman did not justify his election to the caliphate. It is true he was rich and generous, had assisted Muḥammad and the religion by pecuniary sacrifices, and that he prayed and fasted often, and was a man of amiable and soft manners. He was, however, not a man of spirit, and was greatly enfeebled by old age. His timidity was such that when placed on the pulpit he knew not how to commence

> his sermon. … Marwan, in reality governed the country, only allowing the title of Caliph to 'Uthmān.[6]

Furthermore, when 'Ali was finally enthroned after Caliph 'Uthmān, the Muslim community was no longer a single entity like it had before – and many notable companions had passed away. Most of the remaining companions of the Prophet in 'Ali's time had been children when the Prophet was alive. Many of the Muslims, then, were new converts, that is *tābi'ūn* (students and followers of the companions).

Unfortunately, some of the remaining notable *ṣaḥābah* (companions), including Ṭalḥah, Zubair, and 'Āishah, formed an antagonistic party against 'Ali. Both sides waged serious war against each other in the Battle of Camel. The two eminent companions, Ṭalḥah and Zubair, fell in the battle. 'Āishah was escorted back to Madīnah.

When Ṭalḥah and Zubair's forces were overpowered, for 'Ali to settle down and concentrate on the affairs of the caliphate, Mu'āwiyah (a long-time governor of Syria appointed by 'Umar) became another staunch rebel, refusing to recognise 'Ali as the new caliph. 'Ali removed all the existing governors, but he was unable to remove Mu'āwiyah. This led to another terrible war. During the Battle of Siffin, thousands more Muslims died.

To add insult to injury, some Muslims on the side of 'Ali seceded and formed the first Muslim sect, known as the Khawārij (Khārijites). Members of this same sect later assassinated 'Ali in 661 CE, while Mu'āwiyah (of the same Umayyad clan as 'Uthmān) enthroned himself as caliph over all Muslims. Through him, hereditary leadership started, and thus the Umayyad Dynasty was firmly established.

The remaining few loyalists of 'Ali, especially the Banū Hāshim (the clan of 'Ali and the Prophet), refused to recognise Mu'āwiyah as their leader. Instead, they enthroned the first son of 'Ali, Ḥasan, as caliph after his father. But the control of Mu'āwiyah extended across the majority of the provinces. He threatened Ḥasan and schemed against him to withdraw, demanding that Ḥasan recognise him alone. Ḥasan ruled over his few loyalists for six months and then voluntarily withdrew.

Worse still, Mu'āwiyah's first son, Yazīd, felt that the existence of Ḥasan was a threat to his becoming the next caliph after his father; hence, Ḥasan was poisoned to death in 680 CE. This incident, together with everything mentioned above, stirred the emotion and sympathy of 'Ali's loyalists.

A most tragic end befell the second son of 'Ali, Ḥusayn. Of course, the plan of Yazīd to succeed his father (Mu'āwiyah) was realised in 683 CE. However, the fact that Ḥusayn was the son of 'Ali and the grandson of the Prophet truly threatened Yazīd.

During the caliphate of 'Ali, Kufa was his administrative capital. Mu'āwiyah changed the capital to Damascus during his reign. When Yazīd succeeded his father, the Kufans sent their support to the second son of 'Ali, Ḥusayn, who was around 54 years of age, to come and take up the leadership in Kufa (the former capital of his father's caliphate). On his way to Kufa from Madīnah, with only two hundred souls (relatives, friends, and a few supporters), Yazīd's forces, under 'Umar b. Sa'd, met Ḥusayn at a place called Karbala (25 miles (70 kilometres) north of Kufa) on 1 Muḥarram 61 AH/680 CE.

Finding himself in a state of dilemma for three days without access to water and with no more support received from the Kufans who had sent for him, Ḥusayn and his seventy-two men had to fight Yazīd's thousands of soldiers. Thus, Ḥusayn, grandson of the Prophet and son of 'Ali and Fāṭimah, was mercilessly killed on 10 Muḥarram 61 AH/10 October 680 CE. He was killed together with all his male family members except for a son who carried no weapon. This son was 'Ali al-Aṣghar, who was later given the appellation 'Ali Zayn al-'Ābidīn (i.e. Ornament of God's Servants). During the battle, this 'Ali was sick and lying down in a tent without any weapon in his possession. He was, therefore, left untouched. But he was brought to attend the caliph's court in Damascus along with the captured women. He was later released and went to Madīnah.[7] The other three sons of Husayn, 'Ali al-Akbar, Ja'far, and 'Abdullāh, were massacred.

This incident actually revived, and then permanently cemented, the idea of Shi'ism. Of course, the group had already declared themselves as Shī'a before this incident, but they had not been as strong as the event at Karbala made them to be. 'The blood of Husain even more than that of his father proved to be the seed of the Shi'ites.[8] 'Indeed shi'aism was re-born on the tenth of Muḥarram. Karbala's tragic scene gave the Shi'ah a battle cry for unity, organisation and revenge. The first ten days of Muḥarram gave them the national days for lamentation,'[9] as a mark of honour for the remembrance of Ḥusayn.

The strong love and affection of the household of 'Ali displayed through the various Shi'ite revolts added to their hatred and persecution by almost every successive Umayyad and Abbasid caliph. The Shī'a, together with other Muslims (non-supporters of these rulers), were persecuted by these caliphs indiscriminately. According to Amir 'Ali, 'The Umayyad ruled with the free help of the sword and poison. They sacked Medina, and drove the children of the Helpers (Anṣār) into exile in far away land.'[10] 'This general hostility led the Shi'ites to the adoption of the principle of dissimulation (*taqiyyah*)'[11] as one of their doctrines. The hostility of almost every successive Umayyad and Abbasid caliph was the result of the challenges posed by 'Ali's descendants and their supporters, as various revolts and abortive military actions were organised against the Umayyah and Abbasid caliphs.

After Yazīd died in 684 CE, his minor son, Marwān II, was declared as caliph in Damascus. The fact that Arabs were not accustomed to choosing a minor as a leader led the supporters of Ḥusayn in Kufa to organise a revolt against Umayyad, probably thinking that such alien minor status would weaken the government. There was a military action led by Sulaimān b. Ṣuraḍ al-Khuzā'ī. Sulaimān had been a long-standing supporter of 'Ali b. Abi Ṭālib. He had fought at 'Ali's side at the Battle of Siffin. He was in his sixties when Ḥusayn was killed. So, his house was a regular meeting place for 'Ali's party.[12] According to Watt,[13] the Shi'ites' aims for the war were to avenge the death of Ḥusayn, who was killed at Karbala, and to practically demonstrate their repentance for their betrayal of Ḥusayn, for leaving him to his fate at Karbala. These people, around four thousand men, were defeated by the Umayyad in 685 CE, who killed most of them and almost all of their leaders. They were known as *Tawwābūn* (the Penitents), they claimed to repent for their betrayal of Ḥusayn.

Up to this time, the idea of Shi'ism had been purely an Arab affair. In 64 AH/684 CE or 65 AH/685 CE, al-Mukhtār b. Abi 'Ubayd al-Thaqafi, a strong supporter of Ḥusayn, wanted to avenge Ḥusayn's death but got no support from Ḥusayn's only remaining son, 'Ali Zayn al-'Ābidīn. Zayn al-'Ābidīn did not want to participate in politics after what he had witnessed at Karbala.[14] He therefore refused to give his support to al-Mukhtār. Al-Mukhtār then turned to another son of 'Ali from another wife (not from Fāṭimah). This woman, Khawla bint Ja'far, was from Banū Ḥanīfah. The son she'd had with 'Ali was known as Muḥammad b. al-Ḥanafiyyah (surnamed after the clan of his mother). This means that Ibn al-Ḥanafiyyah was not a grandson of the Prophet. He gave his consent for the revolt but did not participate.

Al-Mukhtār, therefore, mobilised the *mawāli* (the non-Arab converts to Islam), who had long been treated as second-class citizens and who now felt honoured to join al-Mukhtār. His movement was known as the Kaysāniyyah. He was able to gain control of Kufa for a short period, less than two years. He was killed in a war between him and the governor of Iraq, Mus'ab, for Mukhtār's refusal to recognise Zubair, who had declared himself as caliph in Ḥijāz (Makkah and Madīnah). The governor of Iraq, Mus'ab, was a brother of this caliph. At this time, Shi'ism was not limited to a particular line of imams, as all of 'Ali's sons were equal claimants to the imamate, whether or not they were grandsons of the Prophet through Fāṭimah.[15]

According to Dr Karim Douglas Crow, two immediate consequences came out of Ḥusayn's death: (1) the *Tawwābūn*, or the movement of the Penitents, which was purely an Arab phenomenon, and (2) the Kaysāniyyah movement of al-Mukhtār, consisting of both Arabs and non-Arabs (*mawāli*, sing. *mawla*), and especially Persians, which gave the Shī'a, as a whole, a wider appeal.[16]

'The movement of the *Tawwābūn* and Mukhtār mark the coming of a spirit which would make sectarianism possible. But the Shī'a was not yet a sect; there can as yet be no division of Islam between Shiʿite and Sunni. Shīʿa and Uthmaniyya were merely positions with regard to the imamate not comprehensive division of the faithful.'[17]

In addition, in 122 AH/740 CE, Zayd b. ʿAli Zayn al-ʿĀbidīn led a revolt against Umayyad and was instantly massacred. His death prepared the ground for other sectarian beliefs. Another revolt was organised in 145 AH /762 CE in Madīnah by the great-grandson of Ḥasan called Muḥammad b. ʿAbdullāh al-Nafs al-Zaqiyyah ('the pure soul'). Almost at the same time, al-Nafs al-Zakiyyah's brother Ibrāhīm led another revolt in Basra. All the revolts were crushed by Abbasid Caliph al-Manṣūr, and the leaders were put to death.

The entire history of the Shīʿa is steeped in various frustrations and misfortunes. This is what probably made ʿAllāmah Muḥammad Ḥusayn Ṭabaṭabā'i lament as follows: 'Several times the descendants of the Prophet ... rebelled against the injustice of the government, but each time they were defeated and usually lost their lives.'[18]

According to Andrew J. Newman, Caliph Harūn al-Rahīd took the seventh imam, Mūsā, to Iraq. Mūsā was imprisoned in Basra and Baghdad, where he finally died by being poisoned. ʿAli b. Muḥammad, the tenth imam, was under house arrest at Samarra throughout the reign of Caliph al-Muʿtazz. He died in Samarra. Ḥasan al-Askari, the eleventh imam, remained under house arrest nearly all his life.[19] To add to the frustrations and misfortunes, suffice it to say that every successive Shiʿite imam met a tragic end. Sheikh aṣ-Ṣadūq ibn Bābawayh and Waheed Akhtar list these imams and their respective deaths as follows:[20]

- ʿAli b. Abi Ṭālib, assassinated by the Khārijite ʿAbd al-Raḥmān b. Muljam
- Ḥasan b. ʿAli, poisoned by Muʿāwiyah, or by Yazīd through his wife, Jaʿda
- Ḥusayn b. ʿAli, murdered at Karbala by Sinān b. Anas al-Nakhaʿi
- ʿAli b. Ḥusayn (Zayn al-ʿĀbidīn), poisoned by Hishām through Walīd

- Muḥammad al-Bāqir, poisoned by Hishām's nephew Ibrāhīm
- Ja'far al-Ṣādiq, poisoned by Caliph al-Manṣūr
- Mūsā al-Kāzim, poisoned in prison by Caliph Harūn al-Rashīd
- 'Ali al-Riḍa b. Mūsā, poisoned by al-Ma'mūn
- Muḥammad al-Taqī, poisoned by al-Mu'tasim
- 'Ali al-Naqi al-Hādī, poisoned by Mu'tazz or Mutawakkil
- al-Ḥasan b. 'Ali al-Askari, poisoned by Mu'tamid
- Muḥammad al-Mahdi, disappeared into occultation.

The above misfortunes baffled some companions of the sixth Shi'ite imam, Ja'far al-Ṣādiq. They asked him why those calamities had befallen the imams despite their claim to infallibility, quoting Qur'anic verse: '*And whatever misfortune that befalls you is the consequence of what your own hands have wrought*' (*al-Shūra* 42:30). Imam Ja'far al-Ṣādiq replied, 'The Messenger of God used to turn in repentance to God day and night without any sin. God usually favours his friends with misfortune as to later reward them for the tribulations without any sin on their part.'[21]

The early Shī'a were divided into numerous other factions, such as the Nusayriyyah (Nusayris), Assassiyyah (Assassins), Druziyyah (Druze), Kaysāniyyah (Kaysānis), Zaydiyyah (Zaydis), Qarmatiyyah (Qarmatians), Ithna 'Ashariyyah (Twelvers), Sab'iyyah (Seveners, or Ismā'īliyyah), and Ghulāt (extremists).

Out of all of these, only three remain in existence today, namely the orthodox Ithna 'Ashariyyah (the Twelvers), also known as Imāmiyyah, who constitute the majority; the Zaydiyyah; and the Ismā'īliyyah (the Seveners). The extremists (*Ghulāt*), though not in existence, were a sect that had gone so far as to declare that Gabriel (Jibrīl) mistook 'Ali for Muḥammad when he called him to his prophetic mission.[22] These extremists were absorbed by other sects.

The Imāmiyyah Shī'a (the Twelvers) remains as the majority Muslim faction in Iran, Iraq, Bahrain, and Lebanon. They have a considerable number of members in India, Pakistan, Saudi Arabia, Kuwait, Qatar, and other Gulf states, as well as in some countries that broke away from the former USSR. A few Imāmiyyah are also found in some West African countries today, like Nigeria and Ghana. The Ismā'īli branch is prominent in India, Pakistan, and East Africa, while the Zaydiyyah sect largely exists in North Yemen.[23] The doctrines of the main body of Twelvers are the official doctrines of Iran.

Genealogy of the Twelve Imams

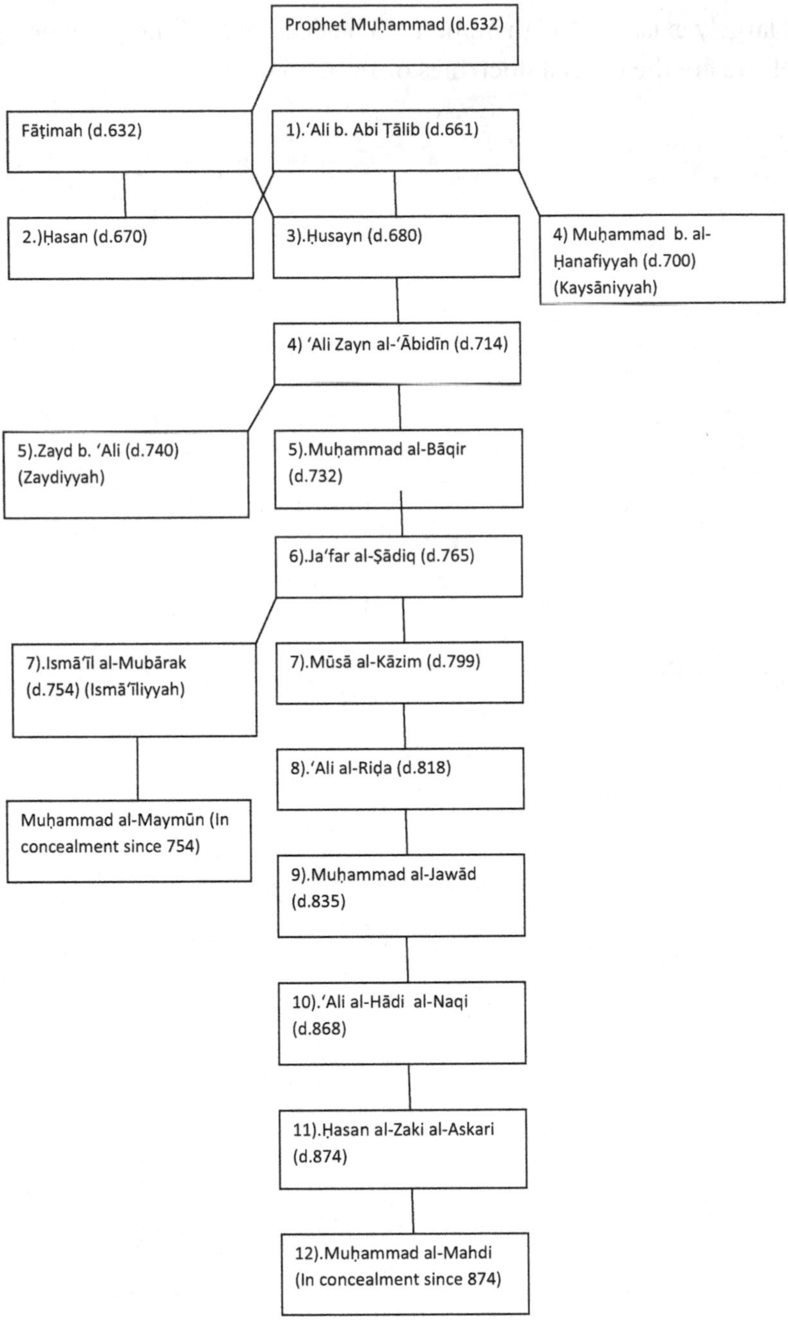

The Kaysāniyyah

It was mentioned above that the death of Ḥusayn at Karbala marked a turning point in the history of the Shīʿa. The Kufan Arabs, with a few others from other cities like Basra, formed the *Tawwābūn*, the Penitents, most of whose members were killed by the Umayyad. After them came an eminent Arab, al-Mukhtār b. Abi ʿUbayd al-Thaqafi, who claimed to seek revenge for Ḥusayn's death. He knew he could not achieve his aim without the strong support of ʿAli's descendants, so he petitioned Ḥusayn's son ʿAli Zayn al-ʿĀbidīn for his support. The son of Ḥusayn had lain sick in a tent at Karbala, witnessing the horrific assassination of his father and other family members.[24] He denied al-Mukhtār's request for support.

In order to carry on with his ambition, al-Mukhtār then turned to another son of ʿAli b. Abi Ṭālib, Muḥammad b. al-Ḥanafiyyah. As mentioned previously, his mother was Khawlah bint Jaʿfar,[25] a woman from Banū Ḥanīfah (i.e. a Hanafite woman), and therefore he was surnamed by his mother's clan as Ibn al-Ḥanafiyyah. Muḥammad b. al-Ḥanafiyyah lived in Madīnah. He gave his consent to al-Mukhtār but did not participate in the revolts occurring in Kufa in his own name. And he never ascended to the ruling position for which al-Mukhtār's movement prepared him. Al-Mukhtār became the self-appointed trustee of Ibn al-Ḥanafiyyah, declaring him to be the Mahdi (i.e. rightly guided) as opposed to the two wrongly guided caliphs: the Umayyad caliph in Damascus and the rival caliph Ibn al-Zubayr in Ḥijāz.[26]

In order to gain a large followership, in addition to the support received from the Arabs, al-Mukhtār invited the Persian converts and other *mawāli* (non-Arabs) to join him. The *mawāli*, who were previously considered to be ordinary nonentities, now felt honoured and joined him *en masse*. This provided al-Mukhtār with great assistance in capturing Kufa from its governor in 66 AH/685 CE. He took control of Kufa for more than a year. He assassinated all those involved in the massacre of Ḥusayn at Karbala. However, after a year, the governor of Basra, a brother of Caliph Ibn al-Zubayr in Ḥijāz, sent out a large number of his troops from Basra. Al-Mukhtār was assassinated by these troops on 14 Ramaḍān 61 AH/3 April 689 CE.[27]

Muḥammad b. al-Ḥanafiyyah, whose name was used for the short-lived successful revolt, kept aloof throughout. He did not travel to Kufa to take up the leadership proclaimed in his name even though people were expecting him for over a year. He lived a peaceful life, and died in Madīnah in 81 AH/700 CE.[28]

This movement of al-Mukhtār became known as Kaysāniyyah. This name was perhaps derived from Kaysān Abu 'Amra, the chief bodyguard of the leader of the *mawāli* under al-Mukhtār.[29] Arzina Lalani suggests that the name was derogatively applied to this movement by al-Mukhtār's opponents to discredit his followers as the followers of his bodyguard. If it wasn't derogatory, perhaps it suggested the importance this movement attached to the *mawāli*, who were elevated from their former debased status as a result of the movement.[30] The relevance, achievement, and significance of Kaysāniyyah to Shi'ism is as follows:

Firstly, al-Mukhtār's invitation to the *mawāli*, and the new eminent status they acquired (as opposed to their former debased status), gave Shi'ism strong footing among these non-Arabs, especially the Persians, who are today the champions of Shi'ism throughout the world.

Secondly, it has been previously discussed that the Shī'a, led by various descendants of 'Ali, constantly organised and staged revolts and military actions that led to the tragic death of many of their leaders. But for the first time in history, the Shi'ites were able to establish a government, however short-lived. Besides, the objective and effort of the *Tawwābūn* (the Penitents) to avenge the death of Ḥusayn was easily accomplished by the Kaysāni government.

Thirdly, whereas the Khārijites prepared various doctrines for the numerous Muslim factions, some Shi'ite doctrines, especially on the expected Mahdi, in addition to a few others, originated from the Kaysāniyyah. That is, after the death of Muḥammad b. al-Ḥanafiyya, a group of Kaysāniyyah started the doctrine of the disappearance of Ibn al-Ḥanafiyyah, especially the followers of Abu Karīb (or Kurayb) al-Darīr (the Karībiyya or Kuraybiyya).[31]

These people said that Ibn al-Ḥanafiyyah was the fourth imam (after ʿAli, Ḥasan, and Ḥusayn) as well as the promised Mahdi. He had gone into occultation (*ghaybah*) in Raḍwa Mountain north of Madīnah, being guarded by lions and tigers and being fed by mountain goats. They said that in future he will return victorious, gather his followers around him, destroy Shiʿism's enemies, establish true Islam, fill the whole earth with justice, and reappear one day as the expected Mahdi. The poets among the people helped to spread this belief quickly, especially Kuthayyir and al-Sayyid al-Ḥimyari. Al-Ḥimyari wrote, 'There are four Imāms: ʿAli and his three sons al-Ḥasan, al-Ḥusayn and Muḥammad (Ibn al-Ḥanafiyyah).'[32]

In addition, this group believed that the Shīʿa had gone astray for recognising the first three caliphs, and hence these caliphs were all usurpers of ʿAli's right. They also believed in the superhuman qualities of the only four imams they recognised at the time: ʿAli, Ḥasan, Ḥusayn, and Muḥammad b. al-Ḥanafiyyah. Although the Kaysāniyyah was among the factions absorbed by the main body of Shīʿa (Twelvers, or Imāmiyyah), almost all of these doctrines are relevant to two of the existing branches of Shiʿism, including the main body, the Imāmiyyah.

The Zaydiyyah

ʿAli ibn Abi Ṭālib was a caliph and an imam. His first son, Ḥasan, was enthroned by loyalists, but he voluntarily withdrew for Muʿāwiyah. Ḥusayn, the second son, wanted to take up leadership in Kufa but was massacred at Karbala. The surviving son of Ḥusayn, ʿAli Zayn al-ʿĀbidīn, did not partake in politics. His first son, Muḥammad al-Bāqir, also showed no interest in politics. Both lived peacefully, and both died in Madīnah without any opposition to the then Umayyad ruler. These were the first five imams of the orthodox Shiʿites.[33]

Zayn al-ʿĀbidīn had another son, the half-brother of al-Bāqir named Zayd b. ʿAli Zayn al-ʿĀbidīn. This Zayd left Madīnah for Kufa to lead a revolt against Caliph Hishām in 122 AH/740 CE and was massacred. His younger son, Yaḥya, fled to Khurasan (eastern Iran). Yaḥya later made an attempt in Herat (western Afghanistan) and was also murdered.[34]

Therefore, because of the effort of Zayd and his massacre, a sect of Shīʿa preferred him over his eldest brother, al-Bāqir, as their imam. Their simple reason was that any member of ʿAli and Fāṭimah's family who took up arms against an unjust ruler was better qualified to be the imam.[35] Al-Bāqir had made no such attempt. This sect of Shīʿa became known as the Zaydiyya (Zaydis). Their factional beliefs include the following:[36]

- Imams are not protected from sin or errors; therefore, they are not infallible.
- Descendants of both Ḥasan and Ḥusayn were qualified to be imams, not Ḥusayn's descendants alone, as up held by the Twelvers (Imāmiyyah).
- ʿAli had been appointed by the Prophet (as others believed), but to them, the appointment was ambiguous/not clear enough. Therefore, the companions should not be molested or condemned.
- The first caliphs (Abu Bakr and ʿUmar) are regarded as leaders, but ʿAli rates above them and above any of the Prophet's companions.
- An inferior person can be an imam in the presence of a superior person so long as he possesses other required characteristics. (This buttresses their reason for accepting Abu Bakr and ʿUmar as leaders even though they believed ʿAli to be a far better choice.)

The Ismāʿīliyyah and Imāmiyyah: The Roles of the Fifth and Sixth Imams

It was mentioned earlier that the death of Ḥusayn at Karbala was a turning point in the history of Shiʿism. The Kaysāniyyah, which came into existence through the death of Ḥusayn, became the most popular and most influential sect for some time. This was because they remained the first to successfully establish a Shiʿite government, however short-lived.

They were also the first to absorb numerous non-Arabs as members, and some of their doctrines remain relevant today to subsequent factions.

However, as influential as the Kaysāniyyah were, the descendant of ʿAli whom they upheld as their imam and Mahdi was not favoured by many because Muḥammad b. al-Ḥanafiyyah had no connection, maternally or paternally, with the Prophet. Besides, the tragic death of Ḥusayn was a binding force holding all Shiʿites together. They favoured the only surviving son of Ḥusayn, ʿAli Zayn al-ʿĀbidīn, who remains, with his father, as one of the grand ancestors of all the existing branches of Shiʿism: the Zaydiyyah, the Ismāʿīliyyah, and the Imāmiyyah (the Twelvers). ʿAli Zayn al-ʿĀbidīn had two sons recognised by different factions as their respective imams. The eldest, Muḥammad al-Bāqir, is the fifth imam of the present Imāmiyyah, while his brother Zayd remains, to date, the fifth imam of the Zaydiyyah.

Thus, the line of Ḥusayn continued from Muḥammad al-Bāqir up to the twelfth imam, who disappeared in 874 CE. Imam al-Bāqir, like his father, refused to participate in any political activities, concerning himself instead with providing religious and spiritual guidance. He was the brain behind the Shiʿite doctrines of imams as the only spiritual guide of the community, as well as the principle of *taqiyyah*, or precautionary dissimulation, which is still part of Ismāʿīliyyah and Imāmiyyah belief.[37] Although al-Bāqir took *taqiyyah* from the Najdiyyah faction, of the first ever sect among Muslims, the Khārijites, he made it a compulsory Shiʿite doctrine where necessary.

The rise of various schools of jurisprudence, briefly mentioned earlier in the discussion of the Sunni, coincided with the period of al-Bāqir's imamate. He therefore participated by codifying the Shiʿite legal and theological views. 'However, al-Bāqir and his son and successor Jaʿfar al-Ṣādiq interpreted the law on their own authority, without much recourse to Ḥadīth reported by earlier authorities.'[38] This is because, as codified by both al-Bāqir and his son, imams' sayings are recognised as part of the Ḥadith on the basis that imams are divinely appointed as well as infallible. Muḥammad al-Bāqir died around 114 AH/732 CE.

Al-Bāqir's son and successor, Imam Ja'far al-Ṣādiq, made excellent contributions to Shi'ism or Sunnism, contributions that are superior to those of the previous imams except Imam 'Ali b. Abi Ṭālib. Eminent scholars of various factions, including two of the Sunni imams, Abu Ḥanīfah and Mālik b. Anas, learned one thing or another from Ja'far al-Ṣādiq, who was a Hadith reporter, a fiqh teacher, and the founder of an eponymous school of jurisprudence, *al-Madh-hab al-Ja'fari*.

The principle of the imamate laid down by al-Bāqir was elaborated on by Ja'far, who added that humankind permanently needs an imam who must be sinless, who will act as a guide after the Prophet, and who will practise *taqiyyah* when necessary. One of his verdicts was that the Prophet had chosen 'Ali as his successor by obvious declaration, *naṣṣ*, under divine command. Other of his verdicts were that the imamate must pass from father to son among the descendants of 'Ali and Fāṭimah alone; that after Ḥusayn, the descendants of Ḥusayn alone are qualified until the end of time; that the Ḥusaynid imams have both perfect esoteric and exoteric knowledge of the Holy Qur'an and of Islam in general; that the world cannot exist without an imam; and that recognition of, and obedience to, the imam of the time is an obligation of all believers.[39]

With these verdicts was how the institution of the caliphate (of the Sunni) and the imamate (of the Shī'a) were permanently separated. The brilliance of Imam al-Ṣādiq earned him great respect across many factions and among Muslims in general. In fact, various Shi'ite factions switched their allegiance to Ja'fari. Because of this massive switch, a popular Kaysāni poet, al-Sayyid al-Ḥimyari, publicly confessed that he had also *'ja'farised* (*taja'fartu*) (i.e. switched to Ja'far's faction).[40]

Imam Ja'far al-Ṣādiq died in 148 AH/765 CE, and thereafter came trouble when trying to determine who would succeed him. His designated son, Ismā'īl, had died before he did, and, his eldest son, 'Abdullāh al-Afṭaḥ, died a few months after Ja'far. This left the third son, Mūsā al-Kāzim, as the next imam of the Twelvers. The last five imams are the direct descendants of Mūsā al-Kāzim. The last, who is the twelfth imam of the Imāmiyyah, is currently in occultation and will appear later as the expected Mahdi.

In addition, some of Imam Jaʿfar's followers insisted that despite Ismāʿīl's having died before his father, he was still their imam, because he had been designated as imam by his father. Still others did not even believe that Ismāʿīl had died. These groups formed a Shiʿite faction known as the Ismāʿīliyyah. The Ismāʿīliyyah stopped the line of infallible imams at the son of Ismāʿīl, who to this day remains in concealment and will return later as the Mahdi at the end of time. The Ismāʿīliyyah later subdivided into many other sects, two of which, the Bawharas and the Āghā Khānīs, survive today.[41]

It should now be clear to the reader that two out of the three remaining Shiʿite factions are expecting their respective last imam as their Mahdi. Besides, the fact that the two factions (the Ismāʿīliyyah and the Imāmiyyah) owe their origin to Imams al-Bāqir and his son, Jaʿfar al-Ṣādiq who codified most of the shiʿite doctrines make both factions share similar doctrines. The Zaydiyyah sect, who follows another brother of al-Bāqir, definitely has its separate beliefs as the doctrines had not been codified before the Zaydiyyah's saparation.

The Early Ismāʿīli Doctrines

Esoteric Meaning of All Revealed Books

The early Ismāʿīliyyah were mostly Sūfis (mystics) whose doctrines revolved around the religious history of humankind. According to Farhad Daftary of the Institute of Ismaʿili Studies, the Ismāʿīlis believed that all sacred books (revelations) from Allah possess both exoteric, or apparent, meanings (*ẓāhir*) and esoteric, or hidden, meanings (*bātin*). In each generation, only the elites (*khawāṣṣ*), the initiated ones who take an oath of secrecy, can grasp the inner meanings of each revelation, which gives them access to the world of spiritual reality. The common people (*ʿawāmm*) understand no more than the outer (*ẓāhir*) meaning of their sacred book.[42]

According to Ismā'īlis, no one is capable of comprehending the eternal truth of the Islamic mission unless they are initiated into the Ismā'īli (Sūfi) circle. Such members must recognise the Prophet as the first authority in teaching and delivering the message of Islam. After the Prophet, one must recognise 'Ali and his descendant imams as the only source of inner understanding of the revelation. The Ismā'īlis maintained that all the revealed religions (Judaism, Christianity, and Islam) contain the same *bātin* message, only that the *ẓāhir* aspects were changed according to different generations, communities, and circumstances. In other words, the apparent meanings of the Qur'an, such as Sharī'ah, have undergone various changes according to changing occurrences and circumstances of time. But the *bātin* aspects remain eternally constant and unchanging. These are the real truths (*ḥaqā'iq*) of the Book.[43]

One can only be a member of the Ismā'īli (Sūfi) sect through initiation (*balāgh*) and payment of dues, with a strong oath of allegiance (*mīthāq*) promising that whatever esoteric knowledge (*'ilm al-bātin*) is acquired will never be revealed to a non-member. This is the reason why the Ismā'īlis were known initially as the Bātiniyyah, even though they equally up held the *ẓāhir* aspects of the Qur'an.[44]

Spiritual History of Humankind

The Ismā'īlis are known as Seveners because they stopped their imamate at number seven and then tried to *sevenise* every doctrine. They explained that the religious history of humankind had undergone seven different prophetic eras at various intervals. Each era was inaugurated by a speaker or enunciator (*nāṭiq*, pl. *nuṭaqā'*) of a divine message.

Their divine missions contained *ẓāhir*, or apparent laws – i.e. Sharī'ah – with various dos and don'ts. The *nuṭaqā'* of the first six of human history, also known as the *ūlu'l-'azm* (i.e. prophets with resolution), were Adam, Nūḥ (Noah), Ibrāhīm (Abraham), Mūsā (Moses), 'Isā (Jesus), and Muḥammad.[45] Adam was present during the first era; Nūḥ was the seventh *nāṭiq* of Adam; Ibrāhīm was the seventh *nāṭiq* of Nūḥ; Mūsā was the seventh *nāṭiq* of Ibrāhīm; 'Isā was the seventh *nāṭiq* of

Mūsā; Muḥammad was the seventh *nāṭiq* of ʻIsā; and their last imam, Muḥammad b. Ismāʻīl, was the seventh *nāṭiq* of Prophet Muḥammad.[46]

Each of these *nuṭaqā'* had clearly explained the *ẓāhir* messages, but the *bātin* aspects remained unexplained with insufficient details. This necessitated a legatee, or *waṣī*, whose responsibility was to explain the *bātin* details only to the initiated elites of each era. The first six *waṣīs* of the above *nuṭaqā'* are Shith (Seth), Shem (Samuel), Ismāʻīl (Ishmael), Hārūn (Aaron), Shamʻūn al-Ṣafā' (Simon Peter), and ʻAli ibn Abi Ṭālib. These *waṣīs* were succeeded by seven Shiʻite Ismāʻīli imams: Ḥasan, Ḥusayn, ʻAli Zayn al-ʻĀbidīn, Muḥammad al-Bāqir, Jaʻfar al-Ṣādiq, Ismāʻīl, and Muḥammad b. Ismāʻīl. The seventh one, Muḥammad b. Ismāʻīl, is now in occultation, or *ghaybah*, but he will reappear as a *nāṭiq*, as well as a *waṣī*, without any new law. Instead, he will reveal the details of *bātin* knowledge mentioned in all the revealed holy books. The six imams before him were just completers, *atimmā'*, whose responsibilities were to protect and preserve both the *ẓāhir* and *bātin* missions of the holy books before the last (seventh) imam finally reveals the details of and imperfections in the explanations of all the previous messages. There will be no need for any religious law, as the Mahdi, Muḥammad b. Ismāʻīl, will end this physical world after ruling with full justice. He is, therefore, 'the *qā'im al-qiyāmah*, the Imām of Resurrection; and his era would mark the end of time and human history'.[47]

Cosmological Belief

The Ismāʻīlis believe that the existence of Allah predates everything. That is, Allah was in existence when there was nothing in existence: no eternity, no time, no space, etc. Through Allah's intention (*irāda*) and his will (*mashī'a*), He first created a light (*nūr*) and addressed it with the Qur'anic creative imperative *kun* (Be!), thus calling creation into being. Through duplication of its two Arabic letters, *kāf* and *nūn* (*K* & *N*), *kun* acquired its feminine form and became *kūnī*.[48] Thus, *kūnī* (which is the first light created, and is feminine in nature) became the first creature. Therefore, *kūnī* was called 'the preceder' (*sābiq*).

In addition, through Allah's command (*'amr*), *kūnī* produced the second creature, known as *qadar* (determination or predestination), as an assistant to *kūnī*. *Qadar* (masculine in nature) was also called *tāli* (follower). *Kūnī* and *qadar*, according to Ismā'īlis, were identified with the Qur'anic terms *pen* (*qalam*) and *tablet* (*lawḥ*) respectively, as the first two creatures of Allah. From *kūnī*, Allah created everything in existence, whereas through *qadar*, He determined the how, when, where of everything.

Kūnī and *qadar*, which Daftary calls 'the primal pair', are written in Arabic and make up seven alphabetical letters (KUNI-QDR). These letters are together called 'the higher letters' (*al-ḥurūf al-'ulwiyyah*). From these original seven letters, names of all things were created together with those things the names represent. From the same primal pair (*kūnī* and *qadar*), Allah created all the creatures in the spiritual world. *Kūnī* then created, from its own light, the seven cherubim (*karūbiyyūn*), naming them with esoteric/hidden terms (*asmā' bāṭinah*) which are only known to the friends of Allah (*awliyā' Allah*) and the sincere followers of these holy ones, the initiated Ismā'īli Sūfis.[49]

Then, responding to *kūnī's* commands, *qadar* created, from its own light, twelve spiritual beings (*rūḥāniyyah*) with various names like Riḍwān (Guardian of Paradise), Mālik (Guardian of Hell), and Munkar and Nakīr (the two funerary angels), among others.[50] The first three spiritual beings, known as *jadd* (good fortune), *fatḥ* (triumph), and *khayāl* (imagination), corresponding to the archangels Jibrīl (Gabriel), Mīkā'īl (Michael), and Isrāfīl (Israfel), serve as links between the spiritual world and the religious physical world.

In addition to the spiritual world, *kūnī* and *qadar* created the lower world, the physical world,[51] beginning with the creation of air and water known in *'ilm al-bātin* as the throne (*'arsh*) and chair (*kursiy*) respectively. After these two came the creation of the seven skies, the earth, and the seven seas. Everything created in the spiritual world has corresponding creatures in the physical (lower) world: *kūnī* and the sun, *qadar* and the moon, the seven cherubim and the seven skies, the twelve spiritual beings and the twelve zodiac signs, etc.

To the Ismāʿīlis, the purpose of these things is to show that human beings, created at the tail end of the process of creation, are too far away from their origin, the Almighty Creator, Allah. In order to remove the impediments or disturbances and make the distance closer, humankind needs to receive spiritual knowledge and training from above through various *nuṭaqā*ʾ, i.e. prophets and imams.

The Ismāʿīlis were so convinced of their doctrines that they referred to everything about them as ḥaqq (the truth). Their faith is *dīn al-ḥaqq* (religion of the truth) or *ʿilm al-ḥaqq* (knowledge of the truth), the call to their faith is *daʿwat al-ḥaqq* (call to the truth), and their members are *Ahl al-Ḥaqq* (People of the Truth).[52]

The Imāmiyyah Doctrines

The theological opinions or beliefs discussed here are those of the main body (the Shiʿite majority), that is the Ithna-ʿAshariyyah, the Twelvers, also known as the Imāmiyyah, whose theological views are the official doctrines of the contemporary Islamic Republic of Iran.

Belief in the Holy Qur'an

Belief in the Holy Qur'an is a general doctrine for all faithful Muslims. Thus, both the Sunni and the Shīʿa are strong believers in and avid followers of the Qur'an. The difference is that each faction of Muslims interprets the Qur'an according to its various doctrines and understandings.

In practice, the Shiʿites are strict adherents to the Holy Qur'an in its entirety. As the Sunnis believe in the exoteric, or apparent, meanings of the Qur'an, the Shiʿites believe strongly in both apparent and hidden interpretations of the Book. In fact, in the most authoritative Shiʿite Hadith, *al-Uṣūl min al-Kāfī*, Imam al-Bāqir and and Imam al-Ṣādiq both confirm that there is nothing which believers need that cannot be found in the Qur'an and the Hadith.[53] Muḥammad Ḥusayn Ṭabaṭabāʾi, one of the most respected authorities in Shiʿism, supports this view that Shiʿites strongly hold to the external teachings of the Qur'an, like ritual practices and other Sharī'ah injunctions, and asserts that its regulations are valid and applicable for all believers at all times, provided that they are learned through the guidance of the *Ahl al-Bayt* of the Prophet. Applications of these exoteric meanings of the Qur'an are not to be abrogated until the Last Day.[54]

In addition, both al-Ṣadūq Muḥammad b. Bābawayh and Lutfullāh al-Ṣāfi confirm that there is no difference between the Qur'an of the Sunni and the Qur'an of the Shi'ites, but the difference between the two factions is that some Shi'ite scholars believe that both *Sūrat al-Baqarah* and *Sūrat Āl-Imrān* (Chapter 2 and Chapter 3 respectively) are a single chapter. Likewise, they believe that *Sūrat al-Ḍuḥa* and *Sūrat al-Inshiraḥ* (Chapter 93 and Chapter 94 respectively) are a single chapter, and that *Sūrat al-Fīl* and *Sūrat Quraysh* (Chapter 105 and Chapter 106 respectively) are of the same chapter.[55] The Shī'a practically follow and apply all the commands and teachings of the present Holy Qur'an according to their Shi'ite beliefs.

However, in theory, the Shī'a also believe in the Qur'an compiled by Caliph 'Ali ibn Abi Ṭālib, which he delivered only to his descendants. In Shi'ite records, when Abu Bakr Ṣiddīq sought for the allegiance of 'Ali after the former's election, 'Ali said he would not leave his house, except for *ṣalāt*, until he finished with the compilation of the Qur'an.[56] This Qur'an was finally compiled and was kept strictly with one descendant (imam) after the other. Thus, the fifth imam, Abu Ja'far al-Bāqir, says, 'Any human being who claims to have collected the Qur'an in its complete form as revealed, is a liar; only 'Ali b. Abi Ṭālib and the Imāms collected it and preserved it as revealed by Allah.'[57]

In addition, a companion of the sixth Imam Ja'far al-Ṣādiq, Salīm b. Salmah, reported that a man was reciting the Qur'an in a manner not the same as how people normally recited it and he questioned Imam Ja'far about this. The imam confirmed the recitation and said that someone, al-Qā'im (the Mahdi), would later come with the Holy Book written down by 'Ali.[58] The sixth imam confirms this – 'Surely, the Qur'an which Jibrīl brought to Muḥammad contains seventeen thousand (17,000) verses'[59] – whereas the present Qur'an consists of 6,236 verses. The next authority to al-Kulaynī of the Shiʿite Hadith is al-Ṣadūq Muḥammad b. Bābawayh. In his *Iʿtiqādāt al-Imāmiyyah*, he explains what the Shīʿa mean by the additional verses thus: 'We say that so much revelation has come down, which is not embodied in the present Qur'an, that if it were to be collected its extent would have undoubtedly be 17,000 verses.' After citing many sayings of, or conversations between Angel Jibrīl and the Prophet, he concludes, 'There are many such (traditions), all of which are revelations, but do not form part of the Qur'an; if they did, they would surely have been included and not excluded from it.'[60]

The Shīʿa also theoretically believe in another holy book (*Maṣ-ḥaf*), this one of Fāṭimah, the daughter of the Prophet. When the Prophet died, Fāṭimah was deeply saddened. She continued to mourn his death for seventy-five days. Then, within this period, the angel Jibrīl appeared to her, consoled her, and had some conversations with her, which her husband, 'Ali, wrote down for her. The angel came on other occasions, and 'Ali continued to write whatever Jibrīl revealed to Fāṭimah, until such conversations made up a voluminous holy book.[61]

According to Imam Ja'far al-Ṣādiq, there is no ruler who will rule on earth who does not have his name and father's name already written in this book. He also said that he could not see anything for the descendants of Ḥasan in the book.[62] This book is triple the size of the present Holy Qur'an and contains nothing about things considered to be either *ḥalāl* or *ḥarām* (lawful and unlawful respectively).[63]

The book which contains discussions of that which is *ḥalāl* or *ḥarām* is the compilation of dictations of the Prophet to 'Ali b. Abi Ṭālib. This is another important book to the Shīʿa, as Ayatollah Jaʿfar Sobhani specifically mentions in article 137 of his book *Doctrines of Shiʿi Islam*.[64] Imam al-Ṣādiq describes that 'the length of this book is seventy cubits, and it was written by the hand of 'Ali b. Abi Ṭālib at the dictation of Allah's Messenger and everything which people need is described there in.'[65]

All three aforementioned books contain theoretically held Shiʿite beliefs, theoretical because all chances to practise whatever the books contain are hidden chances, at least until the last imam returns. Therefore, Shī'a remain as adherents to and followers of the present Holy Qur'an.

Belief in Hadith or Sunnah

Like the Sunni, the Shī'a also believe strongly in the Hadith or Sunnah of the Prophet not only as a secondary source, but also as complementary to the Holy Qur'an.

- 'And we have revealed unto you the Remembrance [the Qur'an] that you may *explain* to mankind that which has been revealed for them' (*al-Nahl* 16:44, emphasis added).
- 'He it is Who has sent among the unlettered ones a Messenger of their own, to recite onto them His revelation and to make them grow, and to *teach* them the Scripture and *Wisdom*' (*al-Jumu'ah* 62:2, emphasis added).
- 'And whatsoever the Messenger *gives* you, take it. And whatsoever he *forbids*, abstain [from it]' (*al-Hashr* 59:7, emphasis added),
- 'Verily, in the Messenger of Allah you have a *good example*' (*al-Aḥzāb* 33:21, emphasis added).

In all the above verses, Allah clearly instructs all believers to take whatever *wisdom* the Prophet *gives*, *explains*, or *teaches*, or whatever he *forbids*, in the same way they take the Qur'an itself. Part of what the Prophet teaches, explains, and gives is expressed below:

> I leave two things of value amidst you in trust which if you hold on to, you will never go astray: the Qur'an and members of my house hold [i.e. *Ahl al-Bayt*]. These will never be separated until the Day of Judgment.[66]

In the above statement of the Prophet, the words and deeds of the *Ahl al-Bayt* of the Prophet form a corpus which is complementary to the Sunnah of the Prophet. This presupposes that Allah indirectly also gives authority to the *Ahl al-Bayt* to be followed, as they are part of 'whatever the Prophet gives'. Thus, the external (exoteric) meanings of the Qur'an, the Prophet's Sunnah, and *Ahl al-Bayt's* Sunnah all provide messages that are complementary to one another.[67]

The Shiʿite Hadith comprises the sayings, deeds, and actions of the Prophet, as well as the traditions of the twelve imams (from ʿAli to the last Mahdi). This Hadith is the second most important source of guidance after the Qur'an.[68] 'Although, a clear distinction is made between Prophetic Ḥadīth (*al-ḥadīth al-nabawi*) and the sayings of the Imāms (*al-ḥadīth al-walawi*), the two are included in a single collection.'[69] This is because the *Ahl al-Bayt* are not like the Sunni's *fuqahāh* (jurists); they are inerrant imams whose authority cannot be rejected, just like the Prophet's.[70]

In addition, any word or action of the Prophet reported by the companions which is not in contradiction with any *Ahl al-Bayt* Hadith will be accepted. But any word or action of the companions themselves is nothing more than the ordinary statement or deed of other Muslims and does not bind any Shiʿite to follow.[71]

It does not matter whether a Hadith is found in the collections of the Sunni or the Shīʿa so long as it is reported by reliable or credible sources (according to the Shiʿite yardstick) and so long as such Hadith does not contradict any of the Shiʿite doctrines.[72]

In the previous chapter, we discussed the corruption and forgery before the Sunni-codified Hadiths took place. The Shīʿa faced this same problem. As a result, they looked for similar chains of transmission to authenticate the Hadiths of the Prophet and other impeccable imams.

According to the Shīʿa, all of the later problems with the Hadiths were caused by the first three caliphs. These caliphs encouraged the compilation of the Qur'an for fear that its knowledge would disappear and in order to free it from any corruption or distortion. They knew very well that the Hadith, as a complementary source to the Qur'an, faced the same problem, but the caliphs continued to forbid its writing and compilation and even burnt those Hadiths they found written.[73] The Shīʿa blame the caliphs that instead of concentrating on the Hadith as second to the Qur'an, they occupied themselves with the victories of the Muslim armies and the subsequent booty, wealth, and worldliness they received. Only a few of the faithful concentrated on the general knowledge (sciences) of the household of the Prophet headed by 'Ali.[74]

In fact, Imam 'Ali had the privilege of compiling a voluminous book of personal dictations made to him by the Prophet. As previously mentioned, this book was described by Imam al-Ṣādiq as having the length of 'seventy cubits, and it was written by the hand of 'Ali b. Abi Ṭālib at the dictation of the Prophet of God; and everything which the people need is described therein'.[75] That is, the information was being transferred from one imam to the other. Imam al-Bāqir and Imam al-Ṣādiq usually refer to this book, which was shown to very few companions of both imams. Some of the Hadith therein are reported in *Wasā'il al-Shī'ah* by Muḥammad Ḥasan Ḥurr al-'Āmili.[76]

Like the Sunni, the Shī'a also categorised the Hadith according to four ratings: *ṣaḥīḥ* (sound), *ḥasan* (good), *muwaththaq* (reliable), and *ḍa'īf* (weak). Thus, with this system of categorisation, the Hadiths of only four scholars passed the test and rated as sound, 'which in terms of their importance for Shi'ism, correspond to the six correct collections in Sunni Islam':[77]

1) Abu Ja'far Muḥammad b. Ya'qūb b. Is-ḥāq al-Kulaynī (d.329 AH/940 CE), *al-Uṣūl min al-Kāfī* or *al-Kāfī fī 'ilm al-Dīn* (The Sufficient in the Knowledge of Religion), 8 vols.
2) al-Ṣadūq Muḥammad b. 'Ali b. Bābūyah or Bābawayh al-Qummī (d.371 AH/981 CE), *Man lā yaḥḍuruhu al-Faqīh* (He Who Has No Jurist at His Disposal), 2 vols.
3) al-Ṭā'ifah Muḥammad b. Ḥasan al-Ṭūsī (d.385 AH/995 CE) *Tah-dhīb al-Aḥkām or Tah-dhīb al-Uṣūl* (Correction of Doctrines or Rectification of the Statutes), 2 vols.
4) ——— *al-Istibṣār fī mā ukhtulif fīhi min al-Akhbār* (Reflection upon the Disputed Traditions), 4 vols.

Those rated in the second category, compiled between the eleventh and twelfth century AH (seventeenth and eighteenth century CE), are as follows:

1) Muḥammad Bāqir al-Majlisi, *Biḥār al-Anwār* (Oceans of Light)
2) Muḥammad Ḥasan Ḥurr al-ʿĀmili, *Wasā'il al-Shīʿah* (The Means of the Shīʿa)
3) Muḥammad Muḥsin Fayḍ al-Kāshānī, *al-Wāfī* (The Complete).

The Hadiths in these collections are less reliable, especially *Biḥār al-Anwār* (Oceans of Light) by al-Majlisi. 'The [critics] blame [al-Majlisi] for having cluttered religion with all sorts of secondary beliefs, some of which – notably the directives concerning sexual behaviour – cause amusement among today's mocking free-thinkers.'[78]

Imamate (Succession)

The Sunni address their early leaders as caliphs, while the Shīʿa address theirs as imams. Thus, the imams play their roles according to three perspectives: 'from the perspective of Islamic government, of Islamic sciences and injunctions, and of leaders and innovative guidance in the spiritual life.'[79] Any imam who takes up this role must not be elected by humans. The Shīʿa regard succession to the Prophet as being purely divinely determined, not determined by human election as the Sunnis believe – and as the first three caliphs were elected. According to the Shīʿa, prophethood is mostly a matter of genealogical inheritance, that is, passed from one family member to the other, and the Holy Qur'an attests to this: 'And surely We have sent Noah and Abraham, and We placed Prophethood and the Book in their descendants' (*al-Ḥadīd* 57:26).

In another verse (*al-Baqarah* 2:124), Prophet Ibrāhīm is named as imam by God. He then supplicates to God to confer the imamate upon his offspring. God accepts, with a condition that any unjust among Ibrāhīm's offspring would never be named as imam. Most other prophets, including Ibrāhīm, Dā'ūd, Zakariyya, and Mūsā, asked Allah that He place their messages upon their offspring or other family members.[80]

'Lo: Allah elevated Ādam and Noah and the family of Abraham and Imrān above [all other] creatures. *They were descendants one of another*, Allah is Hearer, Knower' (*Āl-Imrān* 3:33–34). From this verse, Waheed Akhtar proves that both Prophet Muḥammad and 'Ali b. Abi Ṭālib are descendants of Ibrāhīm, as mentioned in the verse.[81] This means that the descendants of the Prophet through Fāṭimah and 'Ali are direct descendants of Ibrāhīm. The verse also points to the fact that prophethood is inherited within this family circle, continuing with Ibrāhīm's descendants, which include Muḥammad, 'Ali, Fāṭimah, and the imams.

Of course, the Shī'a believe in the finality of Muḥammad's prophethood, yet succession to such a divine position for the continuation of his messages is compulsorily divine too. In order to follow the path of previous prophets, the last prophet, Muḥammad (pbuh), made it clear on various occasions that 'Ali, who was his nearest cousin and who married the only surviving child of the Prophet, should be his successor.[82] Quoting various Hadiths from the following Sunni sources, Mohammed Shomali claims the following:

- Ibn 'Asākir (d.571 AH), as narrated by Jābir b. 'Abdullāh al-Anṣāri: 'Once we were with the Prophet Muḥammad, when 'Ali arrived upon which the Prophet said, "I swear by Him Who has my life in His hand that surely this man and his Shī'ah will be happy on the Day of Resurrection"; and then the verse "surely, those who believe and do good deeds are the best of men" (*al-Bayyinah* 98:7) was revealed. Later, whenever the companions of the Prophet Muḥammad saw 'Ali coming, they would say, "The best of men has come."'[83]
- Al-Suyūṭi (d.911 AH), as narrated from Ibn 'Abbās. When the verse above (98:7) was revealed, the Prophet told 'Ali, 'Those are you and your Shī'ah and on the Day of Resurrection you will be pleased and well-pleasing.'[84]
- 'The Prophet says, "Wisdom is divided into ten parts: nine parts are given to Ali and one part is distributed among the rest of the people."'[85]

In addition, Ayatollah Jaʿfar Sobhani, also quoting from Sunni sources, proves that both at the beginning and the end of Islamic mission, the Prophet clearly mentioned ʿAli as his successor. According to him, when the verse, ʿAnd warn your tribe of near kindred' (*al-Shuʿarā'* 26:214) was revealed, the Prophet invited his Banū Hāshim tribesmen and asked three times, 'Who will help me establish this religion?' It was only ʿAli who stepped forward on each occasion. The Prophet then said, 'Truly, this is my brother, my heir and my successor among you.'[86]

During the Prophet's last sermon, which he delivered to numerous companions at Ghadīr Khumm, he clearly mentioned that he had left two precious things, one being the Book of Allah and the other being his progeny. He later raised the hands of ʿAli and said: 'For whoever has me as his Mawla, ʿAli is his mawla. My lord, be the friend of whoever is Ali's friend and the enemy of whoever is ʿAli's enemy, love whoever loves him and hate whoever hates him, abandon whoever abandons him wherever he may be. Let those who are present convey this to who are absent.'[87]

Thus, with all the above evidence, Sobhani rationally proves ʿAli's sole legitimacy. To the Shīʿa, it is inconceivable that the Prophet, who clarified many issues and shed light on many more, as well as clarifying less important aspects of life, would leave the problem of succession unsolved. A problem usually solved by all prophets and even reformers would not just be left undecided by the Prophet, the Shīʿa believe.

Moreover, the Prophet was fully aware of the impending problems of his ummah (community), which faced a threefold threat. There was the problem of the Byzantine Roman Empire; there were the problems of the Sassanid Persian Empire; and there was the internal danger posed by the *munāfiqūn* (hypocrites), whose envy extended to include other things than the leadership of the Prophet in Madīnah. Now with such internal incoherence and external insecurity, it was unacceptable to the Shīʿa that the Prophet would leave the community he had struggled to organise to its own fate and just pass away.[88]

Also notable is that, according to the Shī'a, the Prophet said during his last hours, 'Bring for me ink pot and paper so that I will have a letter written for you which will be a cause of guidance for you and prevent you from being misled.'[89] Instead of giving the Prophet the writing materials, 'Umar b. al-Khaṭṭāb prevented everyone present from bringing such materials, saying that the Book of Allah was enough for them. Ṭabaṭabā'i says that 'Umar al-Khaṭṭāb, who prevented the Prophet from providing guidance in writing, did not stop Abu Bakr when the latter was dictating to a secretary about 'Umar's succession to Abu Bakr.[90]

The Shi'ite imams, starting from 'Ali, 'were appointed by Allah and nominated first by the Prophet and then by each succeeding Imām, through explicit designation (naṣṣ)'.[91] Quoting from the Shi'itc Hadith *Biḥār al-Anwār*, Ṭabaṭabā'i says, 'Ali ibn Mūsā al-Riḍā [the eighth imam] has said, "The Imam after me is my son, Muḥammad, and after him is his son 'Ali and after him his son Ḥasan, and after Ḥasan his son, Ḥujjat al-Qā'im who is awaited during his occultation and obeyed during his manifestation."'[92]

Allah nominated the Prophet, he in turn nominated 'Ali, and then 'Ali nominated his son. Each successive son was then nominated, up until the last imam, as mentioned above, and then all of them were divinely appointed, as the chain of nomination goes back to Allah, who first appointed Prophet Muḥammad. The imams were the representatives of Allah on earth and the successors of the Prophet. They were assuredly sinless and were divinely given knowledge of both the esoteric and exoteric meanings of the Holy Qur'an.[93]

The only humans who were qualified for such appointment were the twelve imams of Shi'ism. These twelve, according to Shomali, were mentioned by the Prophet even in the Sunni records.[94] Therefore, 'by early fourth/tenth century, the number of Imāms, was finally fixed at twelve – hence the name Twelvers'.[95] The chain of divine nomination, which made the imams be perfect leaders, now leads us to the next discussion, on the infallibility (*'iṣma*) of the imams.

ʿIṣma – Infallibility of the Imams

To the Shiʿites, an imam is above an ordinary leader because his role, which is all-encompassing, spiritually and otherwise, 'presupposes a comprehensive and inerrant knowledge; for an ordinary person trying to carry out such responsibility would not be immune from sin and error'.[96] The imams are so pure that to regard their *ʿiṣma* as mere infallibility does not convey the real meaning of the word. The preferable meaning of the word *ʿisma* is 'inerrancy' or 'impeccability', not 'infallibility'. *Maʿṣūm* means 'an inerrant or impeccable person'. In this regard, only those holy men who 'fill the place vacated by the Prophet' exhibit such impeccability.[97]

In Shiʿism, *ʿiṣma*, or inerrancy, is not a quality limited to the prophets of God. Other holy people, though not among the ranks of the prophets, may be inerrant. An example given by Sobhani is Maryam (Mary), who was protected from all sin and error and yet was not a prophet.[98]

The Sunni and Shīʿa, as they did in the past, view leadership differently today. Ṭabaṭabāʾi argues that there is no continuity of prophethood but that there is continuity of divine injunction brought by the prophets. No prophet is present today, but there must be an imam to carry out the injunctions of the final prophet. Such is a continuous necessity for human society.[99]

Commenting on this, an eminent Sunni scholar, al-Shahrastāni explains that the Shīʿa affirm that the imamate is compulsory legally and logically, just as the prophetic office is logically and dogmatically binding on all for human guidance. Logically, humankind needs a leader to preserve law, order, and religion, just as they need a prophet to give them law. Thus, preservation of law is as important as its promulgation because if no one preserves the law, it is like having no law at all.[100] To the Shīʿa, those who are to preserve such divine injunctions must be divinely appointed and infallible, like the Prophet who promulgated the law.

What then is the difference between the Prophet, the caliphs, and the early *maʿṣūm* twelve imams? The Shiʿite twelve imams, who were divinely appointed, inherited holiness or inerrancy from the Prophet. The Qur'an reads, 'God's desire is but to remove impurity from you, O people of the household [*Ahl al-Bayt*] and purify you with an utter purification' (*al-Aḥzāb* 33:33).

The Shī'a assert that this verse clearly explains that the *Ahl al-Bayt* (the family of the Prophet) are protected from any sin or error, but especially the appointed imams. Still, it may be argued by the Sunni that all other Muslims who strictly obey Allah in all aspects of their life may be purified by Allah. Ja'far Sobhani asserts that such purification of others is an act of religion-based purity (*tashrī'ī*), whereas purification of the imams (*Ahl al-Bayt*) is creative and existential (*takwīnī*), with creativity and existentiality being traits that are inseparable from the nature of these imams.[101] Such purity or holiness is inseparable from them because the Prophet specifically requested from Allah that such be the case for the first four ancestors of these imams. Together with the Prophet, they are called *Ahl al-Aba* or *Ahl al-Kisa*, both of which literally mean 'People of the Mantle'. They are the Prophet, his daughter Fāṭimah; her husband, 'Ali; and their sons Ḥasan and Ḥusayn. The incident with the mantle happened in the house of Umm Salamah, one of the Prophet's wives. The Prophet covered 'Ali, Fāṭimah, and their two sons with the Khaybarite *aba* (the mantle) and recited the above Qur'anic verse. He then requested thus: 'O Allah these are the members of my household who you have promised me. Remove from them uncleanliness and purify them.'[102]

The Shi'ite belief in infallibility includes the idea that all prophets are infallible. That is, all of the prophets never sinned in their entire lives, whether before or during their prophethood. The same is true of the last prophet, whose impeccability is even superior to that of the other prophets. Mohammad Shomali argues, 'Imams must enjoy the same quality of infallibility. The reason for this is that the Imamate is also a divinely bestowed position that requires high degree of purity and spirituality.'[103] No other human being can attain or enjoy such complete protection from all errors and sins.

Furthermore, the Prophet clearly explains, 'Verily, I am leaving with you two precious things, the Book of Allah and my progeny.' Ja'far Sobhani says that the imams of *Ahl al-Bayt* are rated on a par with the Holy Qur'an. The implication is that as the Holy Qur'an is immune against any error, so are the imams protected from all forms of error or sin. The last part of the Hadith sheds more light on this concept: 'As long as you cling to these two, you will never go astray.' Thus, *Ahl al-Bayt* imams are to be unquestionably followed just as the Qur'an is to be followed.[104]

In addition to infallibility, impeccability, and inerrancy, imams also have unlimited knowledge, which is partly passed from father to son, partly acquired through the reading of secret writings handed down, and partly revealed through their dreams, as they usually receive messages from the angels in their dreams.[105] It should not be doubted that people who are not prophets (as the imams are) also receive divine messages through the angels. The Holy Qur'an, in *al-Kahf* 18:66, confirms this with Khidr, who was not a prophet: 'We had thought him knowledge from our presence (*'allamahu min ladunnā 'ilmā*).'[106]

The imams share some functions with the Prophet, especially intercession on the Day of Judgement. In his book *The Message*, Ja'far Subhani[107] discusses three things concerning the status of the imams:

> An Imam shares some attributes with the Prophet and is at par with him in that regard and the conditions, the fulfilment of which is considered necessary for the Prophet, are also necessary for the Imams. Here are the conditions which must be fulfilled by the Prophet as well as the Imams:
>
> - The Prophet must be infallible viz., he should not commit any sin throughout his life and should not make any mistake while narrating the orders and realities of the religion or replying to the religious queries of the people. The Imam should also be like-wise and the argument in both the cause are the same.
>
> - The Prophet should be the wisest person in matter of religious law and none of the points relating to religion

should be hidden from him. And as the Imam is one who completes or narrates that potion of the religious law which was not narrated during the time of the Prophet of Allah, he [i.e. the imam] too should be the most knowledgeable person with regards to the commands, and rules and regulations of religion.

- Prophethood is a status which comes through nomination by Allah and not through selection by people. A Prophet is introduced by Allah and is appointed to the office of Prophethood by Him, because it is only He who can distinguish between an infallible and a fallible person and only He can understand as to who has attained such a position under the auspices of His blessing that he should be aware of all the details of the religion.

The following is a summary of Shīʿa beliefs about imams as compiled by the second greatest Hadith compiler, Al-Ṣadūq Muḥammad b. Bābawayh:[108]

- Allah never created any human being more excellent than Muḥammad and the imams.
- After the Prophet, people's next proof (*ḥujjah*) of Allah's existence is the twelve imams.
- It is to these imams that Allah has ordained unquestionable obedience of the people.
- The imams are the gates (*abwāb*) of Allah, the road (*sabīl*) to Him, and guides (*adillah*) unto Him.
- The imams are the interpreters of Allah's revelations and the pillars of Allah's unity.
- The imams are free from sins and errors.
- The power to perform miracles (*muʿjizāt*) is with the imams. They possess indisputable knowledge of Allah and are the protectors of the people on earth.
- The imams are the noble servants of Allah who act only at His command.
- Love for the imams is *īmān* (belief), and hatred of the imams is nothing but *kufr* (unbelief).

- Any prohibition issued by the imams is a prohibition issued from Allah; obedience to them is obedience to Allah; disobedience to them is disobedience to Allah; their friends are Allah's friends; and their enemies are Allah's enemies.
- The earth cannot exist without any of these imams, either manifest (*ẓāhir*) or hidden (*khafī*).
- The prophets (*ambiyā'*), messengers (*rusul*), imams, and angels are all infallible (*ma'ṣūmūn*). Whoever denies their infallibility is an ignorant person and therefore a *kāfir*.

In Shi'ism, there are only fourteen great persons who are granted such infallible status: the twelve imams, the Prophet, and his daughter Fāṭimah, from whom the divine status crossed to other descendants. These fourteen, in the Persian language, are called *chahar-dah ma'sum* (the fourteen infallible ones).[109]

Visitation as Compensation for Imams' Martyrdoms

Imams' Martyrdoms

To the Shi'ites, all their imams, except the twelfth who disappeared, suffered one tragic end or the other. All of them are referred to as *al-shuhadā'*, or martyrs, including the last imam, who will resurface later and still die as a martyr.[110] 'Ali b. Abi Ṭālib and his second son, Ḥusayn, were killed by swords. According to Shi'ite records, others were killed by various Umayyad and Abbasid caliphs who poisoned them. That is why, according to Heinz Halm, the entire family, *Ahl al-Bayt*, is collectively called the House of Sorrow (*Bait al-Ahzan*).[111] In fact, Imam Ja'far al-Ṣādiq (the sixth imam) was questioned as to why these calamities befell the imams despite their infallibility. His reply was that even the Prophet of Allah, who committed no sin, used to turn in repentance to Allah, day and night, for the sin he had not committed. He said that God usually afflicts his beloved ones with misfortunes and then rewards them later for such tribulation.[112]

To the Shi'ites, the imams, since they all have knowledge of the unseen, definitely knew that these calamities would befall them, but they still consented to take huge burdens upon themselves, especially Imam

Ḥusayn. But is this not suicide given that they had knowledge of the calamities and therefore walked straight to their death? The Shi'ites explain that it is not suicide, because these infallible ones took up such destinies in order to 'voluntarily take upon themselves a portion of the impact of God's justice in all its severity'.[113] Besides, the self-sacrifice made by these imams in their martyrdom qualified them to take up the role of *waṣīlah* (mediator) with God and *shafā'a* (intercessor) on behalf of the believers.[114]

This doctrine of surrogate suffering for believers' sins is what Heinz Halm calls 'Islamic Christology' given its similarity with the Christian belief that Jesus died on the cross for the sin of all humankind. This concept is different in Shi'ism.The Shī'a explain that the Christians believe in the original sin of all humankind, whereas the Shī'a believe that the imams were martyred on account of the believers' individually acquired sins.[115] The Shī'a ask, given the uncommon difficult responsibilities shouldered by the imams, how a sincere believer can show his or her appreciation to these imams.

Imams' Visitations

In Shi'ism, visitations to the infallible fourteen are part of one's religious duty to show one's appreciation for the various sacrifices made by these *ma'ṣūmīn*. Unlike the Sunni, who consider such visits as sinful, Shi'ites regard visitation as a highly meritorious act.

Visiting (*ziyāra*) the graves of the four imams at al-Baqī' cemetery in Madīnah; 'Ali's rediscovered grave in Najaf; and the shrine of al-Ḥusayn in Karbala, of Mūsā al-Kāẓim and Muḥammad al-Jawād at the Sharīf cemetery to the north of Baghdad (al-Kāzimayn), of 'Ali al-Riḍa in Mashhad, and of the last imams (al-'Askariyyayn) in Sāmarrā has been considered one of the most meritorious deeds of the Shi'ite from time immemorial.[116]

In fact, different early Shi'ite traditions affirm the importance of visiting the tombs of these imams. For instance, one day the Prophet was in 'Ali's house with all his family members. The Prophet's mood suddenly changed and he began to weep. Ḥusayn, a very young boy then, asked the Prophet of the reason for his change in mood. The Prophet said that Jibrīl had just informed him of the calamities that would befall the holy family. Ḥusayn then asked about the rewards of those who would be visiting their graves, as scattered as the graves would be. The Prophet then said, 'These will be men and women of my community who would make pilgrimage to your graves seeking blessing by this act. It will be incumbent upon me to seek them out on the Day of Resurrection and save them from the awful fears of that hour and from all their transgression; and God would cause them to dwell in Paradise.'[117]

Another Hadith discusses the importance of *ziyārah*, especially to Imam Ḥusayn's tomb. One of the followers of the sixth imam, Ṣafwān al-Jammāl, came to the sixth imam, Jaʿfar al-Ṣādiq, who asked whether Ṣafwān used to visit the tomb of Imam Ḥusayn or not. Ṣafwān answered in the affirmative. In turn, Ṣafwān asked whether the imam used to visit the tomb or not. The imam then said, 'How could I not visit it when God himself visits it every Friday night. He descends with Muḥammad the best of Prophets and us.'[118]

From the foregoing and from other traditions in different Shiʿite collections of the Hadith, it is obvious that *ziyārah* to tombs is an integral part of Shiʿism.

During their visit to each place, the Shiʿites supplicate for the imams, cry for their martyrdoms, and curse those caliphs who tortured them. For instance, when Shiʿites visit the grave of the eighth imam, ʿAli al-Riḍā, which is the only one in Iran, they 'loudly curse the Caliphs al-Ma'mūn and his father, Harūn al-Rashīd, the torturers of the seventh and eighth Imāms.'[119]

The same behaviour is exhibited during visits to other Shiʿite holy graves, which are mostly in Iraq. The rewards from pilgrimage to those places are earned by the pilgrim because he has torn himself away from all worldly affairs, his livelihood, and all enjoyment in order to travel and share in the imams' pain of torture, weeping with them with the aim of waging symbolic wars against all forces of evil.[120] In addition, the rites of the pilgrims include, among other things, circling the tomb visited anticlockwise, similar to circumambulation of the Holy Ka'aba in Makkah; reciting specific pilgrims' prayers (*ziyārat-nama*); and touching the grille surrounding the tomb.[121]

There are numerous supplications which pilgrims to the tombs recite. One of them, as reported by Ibn Bābawayh (in his Hadith), reads thus:

> Through you [the Imams] God causes falsehood to be exposed and evil times to be taken away. Through you, God blots out what He wills and establishes what He wills, and through you, He removes slavery and humiliation from our necks. Through you, God takes revenge for the blood of every believer (man and woman) that must be exacted. Through you, the earth brings forth its trees and trees bear fruits. Through you, the sky sends down its rain and sustenance. Through you, God takes away all sorrow and calamities ... through you, the earth, which carries your bodies, glorifies God, and through you, its mountains are fixed in their places.[122]

'Āshūrā'

'Āshūrā' is mostly dedicated to Imam Ḥusayn, whose martyrdom is considered to be the greatest, because 'the tragedy at Karbala consolidated the Shi'ites around their Imams'.[123] Different displays of passion take place from 1 Muḥarram to 10 Muḥarram every lunar year. These periods are always full of activity, such as lamentations, illustrations, and dramatic plays that commemorate the events of Karbala. All Shi'ite-dominated communities partake in these activities in their various communities, 'whether in Lebanese city of al-Nabatiyya, the Iraqi al-Kāzimiyya, throughout Iran, or in Hyderabad, India'.[124] Together, these activities are called *rawḍah-khānī* in Persian, and they are always performed in Muḥarram and Ṣafar, the former of which being when Ḥusayn died at Karbala, and the latter being when the aftermath of such a tragic end occurred. During this period, there is always an elaborate street procession, including crying, chanting, and even self-flagellation so as to partake passionately in the imams' torture and pains.[125] To the Shī'a, all of these activities are highly rewarding; to the Sunni, they are highly rebuking.

Disappearance, or Occultation, of the Twelfth Imam

The great deal of love, high regard, and veneration enjoyed by the founders or leaders of all religions makes many of their various followers/faithful loath to believe that such leaders have died and will never be seen again. It should not be forgotten that when the Prophet died in 632 CE, some companions, including the educated ones, such as ʿUmar al-Khaṭṭāb, found it difficult to believe that he had died. This led Abu Bakr Ṣiddīq, the first caliph, to address the Muslims, saying, 'Whoever worships Muḥammad, he had died. But whoever worships Allah, He remains forever,'[126] and then reciting a relevant Qur'anic verse: 'Muḥammad is but a Messenger. The Messengers have already passed away before him. Will it be that when he dies or is slain, you will turn back on your heels? He who turns back does no hurt to Allah, and Allah will reward the thankful' (*Āl-Imrān* 3:144).

The above is an invocation which causes the serious confusion that usually follows the death of some religious leaders. Their various followers perceive and understand the death differently, ascribe different meanings to the death, and offer differing opinions about the death.

The apparent end to the line of imams at the time of sudden disappearance of the last Imam (*c.*870 CE) created much trouble for Shiʿite communities, whether in Iraq or Qum. There were different opinions about the future leadership. 'As a result, the Shiʿah splinted into more than a dozen different groups and sects. This phase of their history is referred to in Shiʿi tradition as the period of confusion (*hayra*).'[127] This confusion was such that it took Shiʿites almost two hundred years to widely accept the occultation, or disappearance, of the last imam. The various sects that developed as a result of this confusion had disappeared, or later merged with the surviving main body, the Ithna 'Ashariyyah, or the Twelvers.[128] Of course, the circumstances surrounding the father (the eleventh imam) and his son (the twelfth imam), Ḥasan b. 'Ali al-'Askari and Muḥammad respectively, brought about such confusion. According to Ṭabaṭabā'i,

> The eleventh Imām, more than other Imāms, was kept under close watch by the caliphate. The caliph of the time had decided definitely to put an end to the Imamate in Shi'ism through every possible means and to close the door to the Imamate once and for all. Therefore, as soon as the news of the illness of eleventh Imam reached Mu'tamid [i.e. the caliph], he sent a physician and a few of his trusted agents and judges to the house of the Imām to be with him and observe his condition and the situation within his house at all time. After the death of the Imām, they had the house investigated and all his female slaves examined by the midwife. For two years the secret agents of the caliph searched for the successor of the Imam until they lost hope.[129]

Given the above, it is understandable why there was a great deal of confusion that lasted for such a long time. As explained in Chapter 1, human beings are not created to view the same issue in the same way. Some Shī'a may have subscribed to the opinion that the eleventh imam gave birth to no child at all, whereas other Shī'a may have believed that the twelfth imam, instead of being subject to divine occultation, had been hidden away by his father so he wouldn't have to endure being tortured by Caliph Mu'tamid – the torture and persecution witnessed by all his ancestors. Probably that is why the strictly trusted ones were the only persons allowed to see the twelfth imam during his temporary occultation before he finally 'died' at about 70 years of age.

Imam Ja'far al-Ṣādiq had once dismissed the notion when occultation (in early Shi'ism) was first ascribed to Muḥammad b. al-Ḥanfiyyah. Imam Ja'far's dismissal might have added to the confusion. The idea of the occultation of the imam originated from the Kaysāniyyah, who asserted that Muḥammad b. al-Ḥanafiyyah had gone into occultation. This was how Imam Ja'far al-Ṣādiq (the sixth imam) technically dismissed the idea. According to Karim Douglas Crow,[130] there was a discussion between a Kaysāni Shi'ite, Hayyān al-Sarrājj, and Imam Ja'far. The imam questioned Hayyān about his wrong notion regarding the disappearance of Ibn al-Ḥanafiyyah. The conversation went as follows.

HAYYĀN They say he is alive and being sustained (*ḥayyun, yurzaq*).

IMAM JAʿFAR My father [Imam al-Bāqir] informed me that he was among those who attended on him during his final illness and who closed his eyes [at his death], who as well, put him in the grave, and who married his women off and divided his inheritance.

HAYYĀN O Abu Abdullah [i.e. Imam Jaʿfar], Muḥammad b. al-Ḥanafiyyah is, therefore, like Jesus the son of Mary in this community because his affair was made to appear [as if he died] to people (*shubbiha amruhu lin-Nās*).

IMAM JAʿFAR Was his affair made to appear [as if he died] to his friends or to his enemies?

HAYYĀN Well, to his enemies.

IMAM JAʿFAR Are you claiming that Abu Jaʿfar Muḥammad b. ʿAli al-Bāqir [i.e. Imam Jaʿfar's father] is the enemy of his paternal uncle?

HAYYĀN No!

However, even given the above, the Shiʿites still assert that both Sunni and Shīʿa believe in the return of the Mahdi to establish justice across the whole world. To the Shiʿites, the promised Mahdi, who has different titles, such as *Imām al-ʿAṣr* (Imam of the Period), *Ṣāḥib al-Zamān* (the Lord of the Age), *Ṣāḥib al-Amr* (Lord of Command), *al-Qāʾim* (He Who Will Rise), *al-Mahdi* (the Rightly Guided One), *al-Imām al-Muntaẓar* (the Awaited Imam), and *Baqiyyat Allāh* (the Remnant of God), is the son of their eleventh imam, who is the namesake of the holy Prophet Muḥammad.[131]

After the martyrdom of his father, the twelfth imam went into occultation (*ghaybah*), as he had been divinely instructed to do. He selected ʿUthmān b. Saʿīd ʿUmarī, a companion of his father and grandfather, to be his deputy (*nā'ib*). After the death of this man, he continued to select successive deputies: Muḥammad, the son of 'Uthmān b. Sa'īd 'Umarī; Abu al-Qāsim Ḥusayn b. Rūḥ Nawbakhtī; and 'Ali b. Muḥammad Simmarī (or Sammarī). Six days before the death of 'Ali b. Simmarī, the imam issued a letter (this was in 329 AH/939 CE) stating that henceforth, special deputation would no longer be practised and that his temporary occultation (*ghaybah al-sughra*) would become permanent (*ghaybah al-kubra*) until the day Allah grants him permission to reappear.[132] The following is the content of his letter to 'Ali b. Simmarī:

> In the name of God the Merciful, the Compassionate! O 'Ali ibn Muḥammad al-Samarri, may God magnify the reward of your brethren upon you! There are but six days separating you from death. Therefore, arrange your affairs but do not appoint anyone to your position after you. For the second occultation has come and there will not now be a manifestation except by the permission of God and that after a long time has passed, and hearts have hardened and the earth become filled with tyranny. And there will come to my Shi'a those who claim to have seen me, but he who claim to have seen me before the emergence of the Sufyāni and the Cry [from heaven] is assuredly a lying imposter. And there is no power nor strength save in God the Almighty, the All-High.[133]

His temporary occultation (*ghaybah al-sughra*) lasted for about seventy years, during which time successive people deputised for him and consulted him. But now, after 'Ali b. Simmarī, it is understood that the imam's permanent occultation began until he returns as the expected Mahdi. This means that since 939 CE, the imam has been alive, as he will be until it is almost the end of the world. Of course, to the Shi'ites, it is easily possible for Allah to permit a person to live for such a long time, as in the past He caused Prophet Noah to engage in his prophetic mission for around nine hundred and fifty years (*al-Ankabūt* 29:14).[134]

That Allah grants such a long life to a particular person may be unlikely to some doubters, but the Shī'a do not consider it to be impossible, as all religions affirm the miraculous power of God. More so, they believe that the forces and agents that are functioning in our world are not only those that are known or apparent to us; other agents which are physically and scientifically hidden are functioning as well.[135]

According to Ṭabaṭabāʾi, the opponents of Shiʿism criticise this notion, saying that if Allah will later need such a reformer, why did He have to create him thousands of years earlier? Why does He not create him at the time He needs his service? The Shiʿite response to this is that such opponents do not understand what the imam stands for. His duties do not end in explaining religious science and providing exoteric guidance to the faithful. His duties include esoteric guidance, as the imam spiritually directs the inner aspects of human beings which lead them to act. He is really in communion with people's souls and spirits from his hidden position.[136]

Such things are easy for the Mahdi to do because Allah has already given him exceptional wisdom and distinction of speech. This is not new, as Allah endowed John the Baptist with similar wisdom when he was a young boy. Allah also made him an imam at a tender age, as He made Jesus a Prophet while he was still in a cradle.[137] But Sunni scholars like Imam Ibn Taymiyyah sharply condemn this assertion of occultation. According to Ibn Taymiyyah, as quoted by Hamid Enayat:

> There is nothing in the Qur'an and the Tradition to support the Shiʿi claim that the Imamate is one of the pillars of religion. How can it be otherwise when the Imām's disappearance has in practice reduced him to a useless being, unable to serve any of the worldly interests of the Muslims? The hidden Imām has now been absent for more than four hundred years. The anticipation of his return has produced nothing but false hope, sedition and corrupt practices among certain groups of Muslims. Obeying God and the Prophet is enough to entitle every Muslim to Paradise (*al-Nisa* 4:13, 69). By requiring obedience to a hidden Imām whom no one can see, hear or communicate with, Shiʿism imposes a duty on Muslims above their capacity – an impossibility in view of God's justness.[138]

But Shi'ite scholar Ja'far Sobhani dismisses this criticism, saying that there are two types of saints: those known to people and those hidden from the people. Both types are exemplified in the Holy Qur'an by Prophet Mūsā and Saint Khidr respectively. The saint coexisted with Mūsā, yet unbeknownst to Mūsā and to other people until Allah guided Mūsā to Khidr. In *al-Kahf* 18:65–66, the Qur'an makes it clear that though Khidri may not have been known to his people, they directly benefited from his services to humanity. This is exactly the same with the occultation of the last (twelfth) imam, whose description in the *Ahl al-Bayt* Hadith reads, 'Like the sun hidden behind a cloud, unseen by eyes, but nonetheless bestowing light and heat upon the earth.'[139]

The Return of the Twelfth Imam as Mahdi

Iran, as the leader of Shi'ites throughout the world, considers its ruling authorities to be only representatives of the hidden imam. The imam is the true head of state. According to Heinz Halm, 'In Article 5 of the 1979 constitution of the Islamic Republic of Iran, the naming of the hidden Imām – as the true head of state – is followed by the pious wish: "May God speed his return!"'[140]

Of course, both Sunni and Shī'a are expecting their different Mahdis, but this belief does not occupy a central place in Sunni doctrines. In Shi'ism, the imam presently in occultation will return as the expected Mahdi of all Muslims to establish true Islam and fill the whole world with justice instead of the present worldwide injustice. According to the sixth imam, Abu 'Abdullāh Imam Ja'far al-Ṣādiq, when the believers begin to witness the following predicted things, which some believe are already happening, the time of the Mahdi is near:

> The believer, in the time of the Qa'im, while in the east, will be able to see his brother in the west, and he who is in the west will be able to see his brother in the east ... When you see that truth has died and people of truth have disappeared, and you see that injustice prevails through the land; and the Qur'an has become despised and things are introduced into it that are not in it and it is turned towards men's desires; and

> you see the people of error having mastery over the people of truth; and you see evil out in the open and the doers of evil are not prevented nor do they excuse themselves; and you see moral depravity openly manifest and men being content with and women satisfied by women; and you see the believer silent, his word not being accepted; and you see the sinful lying and he is not refuted nor does his deceit redound upon him; and you see the lowly despising the great; and you see the wombs cut open; and you see he who boast of moral depravity is laughed at and is not spurned; and you see young men being handed over like women and women co-habiting with women and their numbers increasing; and you see men spending their wealth on things other than pious deeds and no one opposes or hinders them ... and you see the unbeliever joyful because he does not see gladness in the believer ... and you see alcoholic drinks being drunk openly ... and you see women occupying places in the assemblies just as men do and usury is carried out openly and adultery is praised ... and you see the forbidden thing made legal and the legal thing forbidden; and you see that religion becomes a matter of opinion and the Book and its laws fall into disuse ... and you see the leaders corrupt in their rule ... and you see men eating what their wives have obtained as a result of their immorality and knowing this and persisting in it ... and you see worshiper only praying in order that the people may see him; and you see experts in religious law devoting themselves to things other than religion, seeking the world and leadership; and you see the people living together like animals ... and when you see the tokens of truth that I have taught, then be aware [of the advent of the Mahdi] and seek salvation from God.[141]

According to Sheikh al-Mufid,[142] when the Mahdi finally comes, he will appear as a young man of medium stature, with a handsome face and beautiful hair, and with light radiating from his face. The Mahdi will rise on the day of 'Āshūra, i.e. the tenth day of the first month (Muḥarram) of the Islamic lunar calendar. One of the signs of his arrival will be an unprecedented heavy rainfall throughout the world. The rain will start in the month of Jumad- al-Ūla and continue to the tenth day of Rajab.

The Mahdi will at first stand between the corner of the Ka'aba in Makkah and the place of Prophet Ibrāhīm. The angel Jibrīl (Gabriel) will stand at his right side, and Mīkā'īl (Michael) will stand at his left side. Jibrīl will be the first to give his allegiance, and then he will call out to the people to give their allegiance to the Mahdi. In addition to the numerous angels who will accompany the Mahdi, there will be with him twenty-seven men from the followers of Prophet Mūsā (Moses), seven people from the People of the Cave (mentioned in *Sūrat al-Kahf*), and also Joshua, Solomon, Abu-Dujāna al-Anṣāri, al-Miqdād, and Malīk al-Ashtar. All of them will be helpers and judges in service to the Mahdi. The Shi'ites will be the first to march towards the Mahdi and give him their pledge, trooping out to him from various parts of the world. From Makkah, the Mahdi will travel to Kufa, where he will dispatch his army to various parts of the world.

This Mahdi will try all the Muslim rulers. He will not need to listen to any of these rulers because he already possesses all knowledge of the unseen. His work is simply to pass judgement on all the deserving ones according to their deeds. The judgements will not be based on the present Holy Qur'an, but on the original Qur'an presently under the custody of this Mahdi (the twelfth imam), who will bring such Qur'an with him, whereas the present one will automatically become difficult to be memorised, even for those who have memorised it before his advent. He will set up an encampment, teaching people there of the original Qur'an as revealed by Allah.

The Mahdi will rule for seven days, but each of these days will be the equivalent of ten years, which means that his reign will last for seventy years. During his reign, injustice will vanish. The earth will no longer need the light of the sun; it will shine with the light of Allah. After the Mahdi's arrival, Allah will resurrect all the dead, restoring them to life.

To the Shi'ites, this belief should not be doubted, because a lot of proof is provided in the Holy Qur'an to confirm Allah's readiness, at all times, to restore any dead body to life, as this had been done in the past and the same Allah retains His absolute power. To buttress this idea, the Shīʿa refer to the following Qur'anic verses:

> Did you not turn your vision to those who abandoned their homes, though they were thousand [in number] for fear of death? Allah said to them 'die!' Then, He restored them to life.
>
> *al-Baqarah* 2:243

> Or [take] the example of one who passed by a hamlet, all in ruins to its roofs. He said: Oh! How shall Allah ever bring it to life after death? But Allah caused him to die for a hundred years, then raised him up again.
>
> *al-Baqarah* 2:259

Bara' (Condemnation)

Bara' is the doctrine of condemnation of either the first three caliphs or the multitude of the companions who did not support 'Ali's candidature for the caliphate, or the Umayyad and Abbasid caliphs who tortured 'Ali's descendants. The reason for rejection and condemnation of these people dates back to the time of the Prophet when many of his companions began to display open opposition towards him, especially during his illness. This opposition was based purely on the imamate, or succession. When the Prophet was aware of their activities to take possession of the caliphate from his candidate, 'Ali b. Abi Ṭālib, he took various steps to consolidate the imamate or caliphate of 'Ali, which his companions tactically blocked.

Firstly, according Jaʿfar Subhani, when the news of a Roman attack on Hijāz spread to the Prophet in Madīnah, the Prophet organised an army under Usāmah, who was around 20 years of age, and under whom notable companions like Abu Bakr, 'Umar, Abu Ubaydah, and Sa'd b. Abi Waqqās were to serve.

The aim of the Prophet was twofold. One, because Usāmah previously lost his father to Roman attack in the Battle of Mutah, Prophet Muḥammad (pbuh), in order to compensate Usāmah and raise his morale, chose him to lead the army. Two, the Prophet wished to demonstrate to all companions that capable young men could also lead their elders in public responsibilities. That is, he wanted to show that Islam favours skills and abilities, not age.[143]

These companions delayed the departure of the army for sixteen days, giving different excuses for this, such as saying that the condition of the Prophet was deteriorating or that Usāmah was too young. Therefore, the order of the Prophet was not obeyed in his lifetime. The Prophet's aim is described thus: 'Madina should be free from political mischief-makers, who might indulge in activities against his immediate successor. They did not only fail to leave Madina but endeavoured to forestall every action, which could possibly confirm the position of 'Ali as an uninterrupted successor of the Prophet.'[144]

Secondly, the Prophet made another attempt to affirm the candidacy of 'Ali and the position of *Ahl al-Bayt* in writing so that such document would vindicate 'Ali's caliphate. One day, when the senior companions came to enquire about the Prophet's health, he lowered his head a little and reflected for some time. Then he said to them, 'Bring me a sheet of paper and ink-pot so that I may write something for you, after which you will never be misguided.' At that moment, the second caliph, 'Umar b. al-Khaṭṭāb, broke the silence and said, 'Sickness has overpowered the Prophet. The Qur'an is with you. The divine Book is sufficient for us.'[145]

With the above statement of 'Umar al-Khaṭṭāb, the companions became divided. Some of them said that the paper and inkpot must be brought, while others supported 'Umar. When the room became a bit rowdy, the Prophet, annoyed, said, 'Get up and leave the house.'[146] Subhani claims that many Sunni records[147] attest to this event, although in a distorted manner. After quoting some Hadiths, including that describing the Ghadīr Khumm, Subhani concludes that the aim of such writing was for 'nothing except confirming the caliphate of 'Ali'.[148]

Thirdly, immediately after the death of the Prophet, ʿAli and some of his companions were busy readying the body of the Prophet for burial. As the body still lay unburied, some companions rushed to select a caliph, ʻwith the aim of ensuring the welfare of the community and solving its immediate problems'.[149]

When the funeral ceremony was over, ʿAli and his companions, ʿAbbās, Zubayr, Salmān, Abu Dhārr, Miqdād, and ʿAmmār, received the news of the election. They then protested against such election, but the answer to their protests was that the welfare of Muslims was at stake and the solution to this was to select a caliph.[150] To the Shīʿa, this was how ʿAli's right was usurped and the wish of the Prophet was ignored. If Nahj al-Balāghah truly emanated from ʿAli, then the following is the lamentation of Ibn Abi Ṭālib himself:

> Beware! By Allah the son of Abū Quhāfah [Abu Bakr] dressed himself with it [the caliphate] and he certainly knew that my position in relation to it was the same as the position of the axis in relation to the hand-mill. The flood water flows down from me and the bird can not fly up to me. I put a curtain against the caliphate and kept myself detached from it.
>
> Then I began to think whether I should assault or endure calmly the blinding darkness of tribulation. ... I found that endurance there on was wiser. So, I adopted patience. ... I watched the plundering of my inheritance till the first one went his way but handed over the caliphate to Ibn al-Khaṭṭāb after him. ... No doubt these two shared its udders strictly among themselves ... nevertheless, I remained patient despite length of period and stiffness of trial, till when he went his way [of death] he put the matter of caliphate in a group and regarded me to be one of them. ... What had I to do with this ʻconsultation'? With him his children of his grandfather [Umayyad] also stood up swallowing up Allah's wealth. ... Till his rope broke down, his actions finished him and his gluttony brought him down prostrate.[151]

According to the Shi'ite account, after Abu Bakr was elected, he sent someone to 'Ali to ask for Ali's allegiance. "Ali said: "I have promised not to leave my house except for daily prayers." ... 'Ali gave his allegiance to Abu Bakr after six months.'[152] To the Shi'ites, the conspiracy against 'Ali had started during the last days of the Prophet, as the appointment of Usāmah's army attests, coupled with the way Abu Bakr was hastily elected without consulting the *Ahl-al-Bayt*.

After Abu Bakr was elected, he deprived Fāṭimah the inheritance of her father, saying that the Prophet had mentioned that no one would be his heir, that his inheritance belonged to the poor.[153] In addition, Abu Bakr claimed that instead of encouraging the writing of Hadiths, the Prophet discouraged such action. On his sickbed, knowing fully well that 'Ali was the Prophet's candidate, Abu Bakr called on 'Uthmān, the third caliph, to write a will stating that 'Umar should be his successor. Abu Bakr fainted before the completion of the will, so 'Uthmān quickly put the name of the second caliph down in case Abu Bakr did not survive the fainting, which he subsequently survived. This time, 'Umar did not object to the writing as he had when the Prophet wanted to do the same for 'Ali.[154]

Besides, 'Umar was known for his legal and ritual innovations: his banning of *nikāḥ muṭ'ah* (temporary marriage); his ruling that husbands could divorce their wives by offering three repudiations at once claiming to discourage divorce; his prohibition of *tamaṭṭu'* during ḥajj; his prohibition of writing down the Hadith; his innovation in observing *tarāwīḥ* prayer in congregation during Ramaḍān; his modification of the call to *ṣalāt*; and so forth. All of these are contrary to Qur'anic injunctions and the Prophet's Sunnah.

In addition, the third caliph, 'Uthmān, who wrote the will of Abu Bakr regarding 'Umar's caliphate, became caliph after 'Umar, as the latter had convened a committee of men whom he knew would definitely not favour 'Ali. During 'Uthmān's reign, his weaknesses were made known to the Sunnis, namely his tribalism, his nepotism, his unjust torture of the respectable companions, etc., which led to widespread discontent concerning his person and his rule.[155]

Therefore, on account of the above reasons, the Shī'a disown, reject, and condemn the first three caliphs of the Prophet as usurpers of 'Ali's right. In addition to these three, many other companions assisted them, firstly, to disobey the Prophet's order about Usāmah's commandership; secondly, in making it impossible for the Prophet to hand down his valuable will; and finally, in conspiring with the three caliphs against 'Ali's right to the imamate.

Not only these three caliphs, but also all the Umayyad and Abbasid caliphs and their supporters who frustrated, tortured, and poisoned the imams are rejected, condemned, and cursed, especially when the Shī'a make *ziyārah* (visitation) to the grave of each imam. In al-Kulaynī's Hadith, when the name of Mu'āwiyyah is mentioned, a curse upon him follows straightaway, together with a curse upon his Umayyad tribesmen.[156] But cursing the three Rightly Guided Caliphs publicly has been banned since 1740s. A Shi'ite monarch, Nadir Shah of Iran:

> Put an end to those Shi'i practices which perhaps more than any other aspect of Shi'ism were provocative to the Sunnis: *ṣabb*, public vilification of the first three Caliphs, and *rafd*, repudiation of the legitimacy of their caliphates. These he formally prohibited, condemning them as vain and vulgar words which cast discord and enmity among Muslims.[157]

Taqiyah (Dissimulation)

Taqiyah is a form of precautionary dissimulation. That is, a person who engages in *taqiyah* denies his or her faith, feeling, or belief as a means of self-protection. *Taqiyah* is a kind of calculated pretence to safeguard one's belief when and where one is not able to declare his or her faith, feelings, or belief and instead speaks or behaves in a way that is opposite to one's intention, decision, or belief. *Taqiyah* is one of the compulsory aspects of the Shi'ite faith. According to a Shi'ite Hadith, '*Taqiyah* composes nine-tenths of the religion of Allah and whoever does not use *taqiyah* has no religion. *Taqiyah* is to be used in everything except in declaring the prohibition of wine and the rubbing of socks in *wuḍū*'.[158]

When the Shiʿites know that they are not strong enough to be known as Shiʿites, *taqiyah* becomes necessary. In explaining this concept, ʿAllāmah Ṭabaṭabāʾi[159] relies on the following verse of the Qurʾan to back up the practice: ʻLet not the believers take disbelievers for their friends in preference to believers. Whoever does that has no connection with Allah unless you do that to guard yourselves against them' (*Āl-Imrān* 3:28).

It is part of the Shiʿite records that people asked Imam al-Ṣādiq whether or not the Prophet ever practised *taqiyah*. The imam replied that the Holy Prophet used to practise it before the revelation of Qurʾan 5:70, which reads thus: ʻO you Apostle! Publish the whole of what has been revealed to you from your Lord; if you do it not, [it means that] you have not preached His message, and Allah will defend you from [wicked] men; for Allah guides not the unbelieving people.'

Therefore, we see that the Prophet practised *taqiyah* before Allah assured him that he no longer needed to. Imam Khomeini explains the purpose of *taqiyah* as being for the ʻpreservation of Islam and the Shiʿi School of thought; if the people had not resorted to it, our School of thought would have been destroyed'.[160] In addition, the Holy Qurʾan reads, ʻWhosoever disbelieves in God after his belief – except him who is forced to [pretend to disbelieve] and whose heart is secure in faith' (*al-Naḥl* 16:106).

Ṭabaṭabāʾi explains that many Sunni and Shiʿite scholars agree that this verse was revealed concerning ʿAmmār b. Yāsir. After the Prophet's Hijra to Madīnah, the unbelievers in Makkah imprisoned and tortured the remaining Muslims, killing some of them, including ʿAmmār's parents. But ʿAmmār pretended that he had renounced Islam and was released. On escaping to Madīnah, he told the Prophet of his pretence, and the above revelation came to exonerate him and the like who pretended not to be Muslims in the face of extreme danger.[161]

But is this not opposed to the bravery and courage in the face of tyranny which the Shīʿa preach? The scholar replies that one can only talk of courage when there is, at least, a reasonable possibility of a person's success. If it is glaringly obvious that success is not achievable and one still faces such danger, it is no longer bravery but rashness and foolhardiness.[162]

According to Jaʿfar Sobhani, the above verse might have been revealed for specific occurrences, but it is applicable to general circumstances when one has to defend one's life, faith, property, honour, etc. He says that during the rule of Umayyad and Abbasid, Muslims generally resulted to the practice of *taqiyyah*, especially on the issue of the createdness of the Qur'an. According to him, all Sunni scholars except Aḥmad b. Ḥanbal outwardly accepted the edict of Ma'mūn.[163]

In addition, Sobhani points to the seemingly unending persecution and torture faced by the followers of *Ahl al-Bayt* throughout the course of history, especially during the Umayyad and Abbasid caliphates. He says that if anyone is to be blamed for practising *taqiyyah*, why not blame those rulers who inflicted terrible unjust punishments on the followers of *Ahl al-Bayt* instead of criticising the Shiʿites?[164]

Nikāḥ Mutʿah (Temporary Marriage)

One of the most controversial Shīʿa doctrines is *nikāḥ mutʿah*. According to the Shīʿa, *mutʿah* is a contract of temporary marriage between a man and woman, for which the amount of money to be paid as a dowry to the woman and the duration of the marriage are specified. These are mutually agreed upon by the man and the woman before the legal bond, or *nikāḥ*, is made. The contract expires at the end of the specified time.[165]

In this type of marriage, the same conditions governing permanent marriage are strictly imposed. For instance, maturity, mental and physical fitness, lack of force or coercion, and payment of dowry are all applied in *mutʿah*. In addition, all the impediments to permanent marriage, such as being related by blood or being already married, are the same in *mutʿah*. In addition, *iddah* (period of time during which a divorced woman or widow is prohibited from remarrying) must be observed after the specified period.

After fulfilling all the conditions of permanent marriage, it is of paramount necessity for a woman during her *nikāḥ* to clearly utter these words: '*Zawwajtuka or ankaḥtuka or matta'tuka nafsi bi maḥrin qadruhu … wa muddatuhu …*' This means, 'I wed myself unto you with the dowry of … and for the duration or period of … ' The man then says, '*Qabiltu*' ('I have accepted').[166] When the period stipulated by the terms of their marriage expires, the marriage is automatically null and void, and the woman must then observe an *iddah* of forty-five days. Any child(ren) born therefrom is (are) legal or legitimate issue who must inherit both parents.

According to Shi'ite scholar Sayyid Muḥammad Rizvi, *mut'ah* is recommended by Islam to resolve a particular problem. For example, when one is not capable of entering into permanent marriage and cannot abstain from sexual intercourse, then *nikāḥ mut'ah* becomes necessary. Rizvi buttresses this argument by referring to a Hadith from the Shi'ite collection, namely *Wasā'il al-Shi'ah*. When Imam 'Ali al-Riḍā was questioned on the practice, he said, '*Mut'ah* is permitted and absolutely allowed for the one whom Allah has not provided with means of performing permanent marriage so that he may be chaste by performing *mut'ah*.'[167] In case of sudden death, the *iddah* is the same as for permanent marriage, while inheritance is based on what was previously agreed upon by the couple.

According to the Sunni, this practice of temporary marriage was approved at one time but was later prohibited forever, during 'Umar's caliphate. To the Shī'a, there was never a time in the history of Islam when *mut'ah* was prohibited, and hence the practice of *muṭ'ah* is permitted by the Holy Qur'an. The Shi'ites rely on the interpretation of the following verse in putting forth this claim: 'And those of whom you seek repose (by marrying them) [i.e. *famastamta'tunbihi*] for a specific period of time, give unto them their portion as a duty' (*al-Nisā'* 4:24).

To buttress their interpretation of this verse, the Shī'a quote many traditions of the Prophet[168] and many opinions of reputable Sunni scholars.[169]

Despite the Shī'a's quoting from the Qur'an and the Sunnah, the Sunni believe that *mut'ah* is the equivalent of fornication. How can someone marry for only few months or years and then divorce? Such a man may later, after the expiration of the first *mut'ah*, feel that he needs another woman, so he may remarry for a few months or years and then get another divorce. He can continue to flirt with as many women as he wishes while still claiming to fulfil all the conditions of marriage and simultaneously making a claim of poverty. Where is the chastity and modesty of young women and young men when they may have intercourse as much as they like before they are finally married? Thus, to the Sunni, there is no difference between such practice and adultery or fornication. They see women who engaged in *mut'ah* as being like professional prostitutes who collect money after providing their services to just any man. The Shi'ites[170] explain the differences between fornication and *nikāḥ mut'ah* thus:

(a) In temporary marriage (*mut'ah*), there is a contract binding the spouses as laid down by Islamic law, whereas this is not the case in fornication.
(b) A child born of fornication bears the stigma of illegitimacy and is not entitled to inherit its parents, whereas a child born in *mut'ah* is legitimate and entitled to inherit its parents.
(c) In fornication, a woman does not observe the *iddah* period, whereas in *mut'ah* wedlock, it is mandatory for her to observe the specific *iddah* period.
(d) Fornication is prohibited by almost all religions, and more sternly by Islam, but *mut'ah* has been legalised and is permitted in the Islamic context provided it is observed and contracted according to the dictates of Sharī'ah.

The Shī'a assert that the traditions upon which the Sunni rely are full of personal expressions of the companions, especially 'Umar al-Khaṭṭāb. Their conclusion is that if *nikāḥ mut'ah* were to be abolished, it must necessarily have been abolished during the period of the Prophet, not the period of 'Umar, in whose caliphate they do not believe. The Shi'ites quote many Hadiths reported by their imams to buttress their argument.

The Shi'ites believe that *mut'ah* was already practised between the commencement of the prophetic mission and the Prophet's Hijra to Madīnah. Muslims who could afford it used to practise *mut'ah* alongside permanent marriage. The Shī'a cite the example of the temporary marriage between Zubayr al-Ṣaḥābi and Asmā', the daughter of the first Sunni caliph, Abu Bakr. This *mut'ah* marriage produced two eminent and popular companions, 'Abdullāh b. al-Zubayr and 'Urwah b. al-Zubayr. 'Obviously if this union were to have been illegitimate and categorized as adultery … it would never have been performed by people who were among the foremost of the Companions.'[171] Muslims practised *mut'ah* throughout the period of the Prophet and up until the second half of 'Umar's caliphate, at which time 'Umar threatened to stone whoever practised it.[172]

Ritual Practices

Differences in the understanding and interpretation of some Qur'anic verses, belief in different collections of Hadith, and following doctrinally varied schools of jurisprudence all account for the slight differences in the practice of Islamic rituals between the Sunni and Shī'a. The following are some examples.

Times of Ṣalāt (Daily Prayer)

Like the Sunnis, the Shi'ites observe the five daily compulsory prayers in the same manner and with the same number of *raka'ts* (2, 4, 4, 3, 4). However, in Sh'iism, *Ẓuhr* and *Aṣr* are observed together, especially at the time of *Ẓuhr*. *Maghrib* and '*Ishā*' are also observed together, preferably at the time of '*Ishā*'. This is the way the four prayers are normally observed during ḥajj (pilgrimage to Makkah), at 'Arafah and Muzdalifa respectively.[173] Imam al-Bāqir, as quoted by Ja'far Sobhani, said, 'When the Sun begins to decline, the time for the *ẓuhr* and the *'aṣr* begins; and when the sun sets, the time for the *maghrib* and the *'ishā'* begins.'[174]

Imam al-Ṣādiq also said, 'When the sun reaches its height, the time for both the *ẓuhr* and *'aṣr* prayers begin, except that the *ẓuhr* prayer must be said before the *ʿaṣr*. You are able to perform the prayers anytime before the sun sets.'[175]

According to Sobhani, both Sunni and Shīʿa agree that in certain circumstances, Muslims can combine these prayers, especially during ḥajj, sickness, stormy weather, or hardship, or when on a journey. The Shīʿa go a step further, saying that without any of those circumstances being present, one can still combine the prayers, based on both Shiʿite and Sunni records. In *Wasāʾil al-Shiʿah*, Imam al-Bāqir says that the Prophet used to pray the *Ẓuhr* and *Aṣr* together, without any reason or special circumstance to justify such.The Shīʿa prove it further that, it is written in Ṣaḥīḥ *Muslim*, 'The Messenger of God prayed the *ẓuhr* and *ʿaṣr* together, and the *maghrib* and the *ʿishāʾ* together, without his being a traveller or in fear [of being attacked by the enemy in wartime].'[176]

Sobhani also claims that when the Prophet was asked why he combined those four prayers, he replied, 'I did this lest my community find hardship [in the performance of the obligatory duties of Islam].'[177]

The Shīʿa agree that the prayers are preferably better observed during their individual periods, as the Sunni practise, but this does not preclude the permissibility of combining them without any extenuating circumstance, as combining the prayers was clearly allowed and practised by the Prophet and the Shiʿite imams. 'The principal point is that the one who prays should be allowed to decide for himself weather or not to join the set of prayers together, for the sake of relieving him of any difficulty.'[178]

Wuḍūʾ (Ablution)

According to the Shiʿites, the Holy Qur'an says, 'O you who believe, when you rise for prayer, *wash* your faces and your hands up to the elbows, and *wipe* your heads and (*wash*) your feet up to the ankles' (*al-Māʾidah* 5:6, emphasis added).

To the Shiʿites, the Qur'an describes only the parts of the body to be cleansed and not how to do the washing. Therefore, judging by common sense and the customary practices of people, it is best to wash both the face and hands from the top downward. That is, the Shīʿa wash the arms from the elbows to the wrists, not the other way round.

The same verse commands the believers to wash both their faces and hands and wipe both their heads and feet. The word *wash*, which the Sunni normally add in brackets before 'your feet', does not appear at all in the verse. This is because in the Qur'anic expression of the verse, between *arjulikum* (your feet) and *aydiyakum* (your hands), there is an obstructing sentence, 'So wipe your heads.' It is grammatically incorrect in Arabic to make the meaning of the word *arjulikum* refer back to *fagh silū aydiyakum* (wash your hands). Rather, it follows '*fam saḥū bi ru'ūsikum* [rub or wipe your heads] and then your feet to the ankles'. Thus, the Shiʿites wash their faces and hands but only wipe their heads and feet in their ablution.[179]

Adhān (Call to Prayer)

The Shiʿite call to prayer (*adhān*) is the same as the Sunni call to prayer except that after the two phrases of *shahādah*, the Shīʿa include '*ash-hadu anna 'Aliyan waliy Allāh*' (i.e. I bear witness that 'Ali is a friend of Allah) twice.[180] In addition to that, after *ḥayya 'ala al-falāḥ*, the next phrase is *ḥayya 'ala khayr al-'amal* (i.e. hurry to good act) twice. The Shīʿa accuse Caliph 'Umar b. al-Khaṭṭāb of having removed that phrase from the *adhān*, which the Shīʿa feel was unnecessary tampering with divine injunction.[181]

Unfolding Hands in Ṣalāt

To the Shīʿa, folding hands in *ṣalāt* is an innovation (*bid'ah*) which is forbidden in *imāmi fiqh* (jurisprudence). Quoting from Sunni records/sources,[182] in addition to their own, the Shīʿa conclude that such an act came about after the Prophet's death.

Prostration

In Shiʿism, prostration should be made upon the earth or upon natural materials except those earthly materials that can be worn or eaten.

Quoting from *Wasāʾil al-Shiʿah*, Imam al-Ṣādiq said, 'The prostration is allowed only on the earth or on what grows from the earth, except that which can be eaten or worn.'[183]

According to Jaʿfar Sobhani, the Companions of the Prophet used to prostrate on the earth or its natural components and not on any carpet or cloth. But by necessity, the Companions used to prostrate on part of their turbans. In order to follow the Sunnah of the Prophet, Shiʿites prefer to prostrate on any natural component of the earth. This belief, says Yann Richard, is what makes Shiʿites to customarily place a tiny tablet of clay brought from a holy place [Mashhad, Karbala, or Najaf] on the spot where their forehead will touch the ground.[184]

Ṣalāt al-Jumʿah

Ṣalāt al-Jumʿah has social and political significance to the Sunni. In Shiʿism, *Ṣalāt al-Jumʿah* is observed at least in one mosque in every town or city. But if no imam is there to lead the prayer, it means that it is not important to observe *Ṣalāt al-Jumʿah*, so Muslims should just observe the compulsory prayer and then go on their way.[185]

Tarāwīḥ during Ramaḍān

The Shīʿa consider the praying of *Tarāwīḥ* in a congregation to be an innovation (*bidʿah*). They uphold that only the compulsory prayers are to be observed in congregation. Both Imam al-Bāqir and Imam al-Riḍā condemned any *mustaḥāb* prayer in congregation as *bidʿah*, saying that it would lead one to the hellfire.[186]

Ḥajj (Pilgrimage)

All rites of ḥajj are performed in the same manner by the Sunni and the Shīʿa. The Shīʿa, however, place more emphasis on visits to the tombs of their holy ones, especially the infallible imams and other Shiʿite saints.[187] This, to the Shīʿa, is highly commendable, while to the Sunni, is highly condemnable.

Human Perfection: An Absolute Impossibility

From all we have discussed in *The Sunni and the Shī'a* so far, it is obvious that, in addition to the cause of natural differences between human beings coupled with the allegorical nature of some Qur'anic verses, three other important seeds germinated to give rise to *fitnah* in the lives of all Muslims, past and present: the political struggle for leadership; tribal or racial sentiment, which today includes national or state patriotism; and selfish interests or personal motives.

It should be mentioned here that political envy existed even under the leadership of the Prophet, as 'Abdullāh b. 'Ubayy and his followers envied the Prophet's role and power. They preferred to be led by someone chosen from among themselves instead of being controlled by people (the Muhājirūn) from another city (tribal sentiment). Some authors contend that the intertribal politics between various Arab tribes were so difficult that the Prophet was unable to choose a candidate to succeed him, and instead left behind various indications that Muslims should make their own choice from two candidates, Abu Bakr and 'Ali.

Immediately after the death of the Prophet, some of these same people, the Anṣār Khazraj, desperately convened a secret meeting at the Saqīfa Bani Sā'ida to quickly elect their own leader, at least over them in Madīnah, so that whoever was not satisfied with the decision could leave the city. After prolonged arguments, during which many expressed their convictions, this meeting finally produced Caliph Abu Bakr Ṣiddīq as the first successor of the Prophet, a decision which today remains as the bone of contention between the supporters of 'Ali (the Shī'a) and the rest of the Muslims (the Sunni).

Since that time, the Shī'a (i.e. supporters of 'Ali) have been relegated to an opposition party, a status which has, all along, led them to attack the mainstream (i.e. the Sunni) leaders as usurpers of 'Ali's right, perpetrators of corruption, falsifiers of ritual laws, and so forth. Although 'Ali became the caliph and imam for a short period of time, after this his descendants and their supporters resumed to their status as the opposition party.

However civilised humankind claims to be today, one of the roles of the opposition party, either in a developed nation or a developing nation, is to point out the loopholes or defects of the ruling parties and then arrogate to themselves excellence or even perfection in order to sell themselves to the local masses. This has, all along, been the status quo of the Shī'a against the Sunni, as their relationship has always been on-and-off between conflict and conciliation.

It is mentioned in the previous chapter that during the articulation of Sunnism, the Sunni *Salaf* (venerated ancestors) unanimously agreed to accept both the negative and positive parts of their history. For instance, the Sunni do not cover up the misdeeds of the Umayyads during Caliph 'Uthmān's administration. Out of the numerous Umayyad caliphs, the Sunni accept that only Caliph 'Umar b. Abd al-'Azīz was upright. It is therefore irrelevant to start pointing out errors to the Sunni, who have already accepted their errors.

The aim of pointing out some imperfections of Shi'ism is not to make criticism of any kind, constructive or destructive, but rather to ask any objective Shī'a to accept the fact that despite the Shi'ite arrogation of perfection, infallibility, impeccability, and totality of knowledge to their imams, these imams were human beings who humanly articulated the doctrines of Shi'ism and who were subject to the same human imperfection they tried to reject, as is still reflected in Shī'a doctrines. For instance, neither Imam 'Ali nor his sons were regarded as superhumans by the Prophet or his companions. In fact, the close friends of 'Ali among the *ṣaḥābah* (Salmān al-Fārisi, Abu Dhārr al-Ghiffāri, al-Miqdād b. al-Aswad al-Kindi, and 'Ammār b. Yāsir) did not know 'Ali as superhuman, nor did other *ṣaḥābah*. If Caliph 'Ali was not known as such, then the issue of transferring anything from father to son would be irrelevant.

On Wilāyah, Imāmah, and Khilāfah (Succession)

The issue of succession of the Prophet by his descendants remains as one of the major reasons for the division of Muslims into Sunni and Shī'a. If this issue had been as important to the Prophet as the Shī'a claim, then he would have solved the problem once and for all. If this issue were a pillar of the Islamic faith, then Allah would have included it as part of His revelation. But it is not one of the Five Pillars of Islam, or one of the Six Components of an Īmān, or part of any other compulsory aspect of Islam that the Prophet must have chosen a successor from his family members. If the Shīʿa claim it is, it also means that both Allah and His Apostle explicitly failed to deliver an important component of the Islamic faith.

Many Sunni and Shiʿite records report the last statements of the Prophet made in the presence of his wives and some notable companions, including Imam ʿAli, repeating what he had already delivered, like his emphases on *ṣalāt, zakāt*, and the decent treatment of one's slaves. The Prophet did not mention who was to be his successor until he breathed his last. How could any Prophet forget or refuse to deliver a compulsory part of his message until he was about to breathe his last? Even more than this, the Qur'an had already confirmed, 'Today I have perfected your Religion for you, completed My favour upon you' (*al-Mā'idah* 5:3), some months before the death of the Prophet. This means that the issue of *wilāyah*, or succession of the Prophet's descendants, is not part of any compulsory aspect of Islam. No wonder he refused to clearly instal anyone until he breathed his last.

Ayatollah Jaʿfar Sobhani says that 'after the appointment of ʿAli as successor to the Prophet, the above verse relating to the "perfecting of religion" was revealed at Ghadir'.[188] Now, if the Prophet had appointed his successor, and this revelation came to bind such election together with all his other prophetic missions and messages, then why was the Prophet still 'scheming' to send notable companions to war before he could instal his candidate or perform his divine assignment? Why were the multitude of companions, and not just a few supporters of ʿAli, not aware of this confirmation? Out of ʿAli's few supporters, some of them, (the Zaydiyyah), who had codified their doctrines independent of Imams al-Bāqir and al-Ṣādiq, agreed with numerous other Muslims that such clear confirmation had never been given. Why are the Shīʿa still annoyed with Caliph ʿUmar b. al-Khaṭṭāb for not allowing the inkpot and paper to be brought to the Prophet at the last minute if ʿAli had already been appointed at Ghadīr? There are many questions raised by the assertion that ʿAli had already been named as Prophet Muḥammad's successor at Ghadīr.

In addition, if the Shīʿa still believe that Caliph ʿUmar b. al-Khaṭṭāb and some of the companions prevented the Prophet from choosing his successor, this means to the Shīʿa that ordinary followers prevented the Prophet from carrying out his primary compulsory assignment. Is this a credit to the Prophet or a discredit to his personality – just for the purpose of defending some doctrines? Consider also that Abu Bakr ruled over the same companions of the Prophet when he unilaterally selected ʿUmar al-Khaṭṭāb as the second caliph. Despite some companions' criticisms of and resistance to ʿUmar's selection, Abu Bakr selected him – and there was no revolt or chaos for the entire eight years of ʿUmar's administration.

If this is what the Shīʿa consider to be confirmation that the honourable *ṣaḥābah* were hypocrites, then how was it possible for Abu Bakr and ʿUmar, but not for the founder of the community, to control these 'hypocrites'? In light of this, are the Shīʿa not telling the whole world that the Prophet was a 'weak' leader? In order to defend ordinary doctrines, the Shīʿa discredit the majority of the companions, thinking that by doing this they exonerate the Prophet, but they fail to realise that they are also attacking the Prophet. All these facts are probably what made Imam Ayatollah Khomeine accept that after the death of the Prophet, 'There was unanimous agreement concerning the necessity for government. *There was disagreement only as to which person* should assume responsibility for government and head of the state' (emphasis added).[189]

Furthermore, Ṭabaṭabā'i quotes a Hadith to confirm the legitimacy of ʿAli: 'Hudhayfah has said, the Prophet said, "If you make ʿAli my vicegerent and successor – *which I do not think you will do* – you will find him a perspicacious guide who will direct you towards straight path"' (emphasis added).[190]

If the Prophet stated clearly that he did not think that ʿAli would be elected and yet intentionally left the matter unresolved, then this causes the criticism of all *ṣaḥābah* to crumble. In addition, 'Allāmah Ṭabaṭāba'i mentions the companions' reason for not choosing 'Ali: 'He was pushed aside from the caliphate on the claim that he was too young and that he had many enemies among the people because of the blood of the polytheists he had spilled in the war fought along side the Prophet.'[191]

Firstly, was Caliph 'Ali the only one who fought with the Prophet in all battles? No. So why were others not hated? Secondly, is it possible that numerous *ṣaḥābah* hated 'Ali but that the Prophet was ignorant of such hatred? Definitely not. Therefore, the reason mentioned by Ṭabaṭāba'i was probably the reason why the Prophet cast the doubt on the election of 'Ali, saying to his companions, 'Which I do not think you will do'. Thirdly, how would the Prophet force a candidate on the people whom he knew the majority of his subjects already hated? The Shī'a are blaming the *ṣaḥābah* unjustly for not electing an unpopular candidate to rule over them. Whereas up till now, the Islamic Republic of Iran, as a leading Shī'i community for instance, still strongly believes in democracy, and respects the popular choice of people in choosing the political leaders.

Besides, if the Prophet's address at Ghadīr Khum, wherein he said, 'Whoever I am his master, 'Ali is also his master,' really means that 'Ali was to be his successor, the interval between that Ghadīr Khum statement and the Prophet's taking ill was long enough for him to clearly instal his candidate without allowing anyone to object to his wish. Abu Bakr and 'Umar took ill too, and installed their successors conveniently before they finally passed away.

On the issue of Usāmah b. Zayd's commandership of the Muslim army, why did the Prophet of God need to devise a scheme, sending the notable companions to war, before he could instal his choice of successor? If they were so fearsome or frightening to the Prophet that he could not enthrone 'Ali in their presence, then they had the power to disobey 'Ali once they returned from war. The Khārijites had unfortunately demonstrated this anyway. Besides, Abu Bakr carried out the order of the Prophet by choosing the same Usāmah as commander, despite the same companions' complaint about Usāmah's age. The companions easily obeyed Abu Bakr, went to the same battle, and gallantly won. Now, the Shīʿa should note that they are attacking the Prophet as being a 'weak' leader because his successors did what the Shīʿa claim was impossible for the Prophet.

Then there is the matter of the inkpot and paper, which the Shīʿa believe Caliph ʿUmar b. al-Khaṭṭāb denied the Prophet so as to prevent him from writing down the name of his successor. This is the same thing as attacking the Prophet's personality. How could anyone imagine that the Prophet would leave such an important matter until the last minutes of his life? Why do the Shīʿa consider the inherent assertion that the Prophet was unable to control the majority of his *ṣaḥābah* as being dignifying to the Apostle of Allah? Why was it possible for Abu Bakr to write down a will and mention his successor, and for ʿUmar to rule for eight years without any revolt from the existing Muslims and the new converts?

On top of this, ʿUmar made a few suggestions to the Prophet which the Prophet rejected. For instance, at Muraysi during the campaign of Banū al-Mustaliq, in which ʿAbdullāh b. ʿUbayy and his supporters were plotting against the Prophet and the Muhājirūn, ʿUmar suggested to the Prophet that he send Bilāl to Ibn ʿUbayy to kill him, but the Prophet refused.[192] If the Prophet then did not have the ability to refuse to implement ʿUmar's suggestion concerning the inkpot and paper, what do the Shīʿa suggest happened to the Prophet to render him thusly unable?

The eminent scholar, Muḥammad ibn Saʿd, in his *Ṭabaqāt al-Kabīr*, a Sunni source which the Shīʿa often quote when discussing the issue of the inkpot and paper, reports that ʿAli was there when the Prophet was on his deathbed, and Prophet Muḥammad (pbuh) said the same thing to ʿAli, asking to bring him writing materials. ʿAli, it is reported, told the Prophet that he would retain everything in memory instead of having him write anything down. ʿAli said he was afraid that before he returned with the inkpot and paper, the Prophet would breathe his last. Why do the Shīʿa refuse to criticise Imam ʿAli for rejecting the order of the Prophet? Why do they blame only ʿUmar al-Khaṭṭāb, while he and ʿAli committed same 'offence'? The Prophet, before he died, mentioned everything he wanted to say, which did not include anything about his succession.[193]

Professor Wilferd Madelung, after citing all the Qur'anic verses mentioning the prophets who were succeeded by their close relatives, concludes, 'In the Qur'ān, the descendants and close kin of the prophets are their heirs also in respect to kingship (*mulk*), rule (*ḥukm*), wisdom (*ḥikma*), the book and the imamate.' Given this, there is no reason why Muḥammad should not also have been succeeded by his *Ahl al-Bayt*. Madelung asks the question that if God hadn't wanted Muḥammad's *Ahl al-Bayt* to succeed him, then why didn't God kill the Prophet's grandsons as He killed all his sons in his lifetime? To Madelung, the fact that God allowed Ḥasan and Ḥusayn to survive the Prophet is an indication of their qualification to succeed the Prophet in his mission.[194]

Firstly, if God had really wanted the Prophet's descendants to succeed him, then He could have at least sent a revelation on this matter. He could have killed Abu Bakr, 'Umar, and 'Uthmān even before the Prophet died. Therefore, if Allah's having kept the grandsons of the Prophet alive is Madelung's yardstick concerning their right to succeed the Prophet, then God kept the first three caliphs alive for the same reason. In addition, the Shi'ites' claim that Prophet Muḥammad, 'Ali, and Fāṭimah are Prophet Ibrāhīm's descendants as the qualification for the continuity of the imamate also applies to Abu Bakr, 'Umar, and 'Uthmān, as they all belong to the Qurayhi clan. It was the Quraysh as a whole who had a connection with Prophet Ibrāhīm, not Banū Hāshim specifically.

Secondly, previous Prophets were succeeded by their close relatives because they were all sent to their tribesmen, including 'Isā, whose religion is universal today (see Mark 15:24 in the Bible). But the last Prophet was sent to the whole world, not only to those of his Arab race. 'We have not sent you except as a mercy to the whole universe' (*al-Anbiyā'* 21:107); 'We have not sent you except to the whole of mankind' (*Saba'* 34:28).

The fact that the message of Islam has been declared universal and everlasting (i.e. there will not be another messenger) right from the beginning has rendered family succession unpracticable. This is why different factions of the Shīʿa, who are still advocating for such, became stuck at different intervals on the continuity of such family succession.

The Imāmiyyah were in a state of confusion for almost two centuries on this issue before arriving at the idea of concealment, or occultation, of the twelfth imam. This is an indication of the clear difference between all previous Prophets, who were each sent to a very small tribe, and the last Prophet, who was sent to all races and all generations until the end of the world.

In fact, Allah has practically demonstrated to all Shīʿa, as followers of the Holy Qur'an, that He is solely responsible for enthroning and dethroning whomever He wishes (*Āl-Imrān* 3:26). When the sixth imam, Jaʿfar al-Ṣādiq, died in 148 AH/765 CE, he had already designated his son Ismāʿīl as his successor. But his chosen son died before him. Jaʿfar al-Ṣādiq's eldest son, ʿAbdullāh al-Afṭaḥ, died shortly after him. Despite Jaʿfar al-Ṣādiq's wish for his son Ismāʿīl to succeed him, and despite Jaʿfar al-Ṣādiq's total knowledge of everything endowed to imams, Allah displayed His supremacy and elected Mūsā al-Kāzim as the imam.

All these things point to only one fact: If Caliphs Abu Bakr, ʿUmar, and ʿUthmān were usurpers of ʿAli's right, then this means they had special power to change the *qaḍā'* (destiny) and *qada*r (decree) of Allah. That is, Allah determined this caliphate for ʿAli, but human beings changed Allah's decree. But when Allah determined prophethood for Muḥammad (pbuh), no human being and no jinn was able to avert that. It is relevant here to remind the Shīʿa of the brilliant explanations and verdicts concerning qaḍā' and qadar explained by the first imam, ʿAli b. Abi Ṭālib, and the sixth imam, Jaʿfar al-Ṣādiq, as reported by the second Shiʿite Hadith compiler, al-Ṣadūq Muḥammad b.Bābawayh:

> Our belief concerning this is the reply of [Imam Jaʿfar] aṣ-Ṣādiq to Zarāra when he was asked: 'What do you say O my Leader, concerning destiny?' The reply of Imam aṣ-Ṣādiq was [as follows]:

> 'The Prince of Believers ['Ali b. Abi Ṭālib], when questioned about the decree replied: "It is a deep sea, do not enter into it." Then the man asked him a second time and he replied: "It is a dark path, do not traverse it." Then he asked him a third time and he said: "It is a secret of Allah, do not speak about it." And the Prince of Believers on whom be peace, said concerning the decree [qadar]: "Lo! Verily, qadar is a secret of Allah's secret, and a veil of Allah's veils, and a guarded thing within Allah's guarded thing, being raised within the veil of Allah, concealed from Allah's creatures and sealed by the seal of Allah. Among the things within the knowledge of Allah, it has priority (over all others). Allah has exonerated his slaves from its knowledge, and elevated it beyond the ambit of their perception and reason. … It does not befit anyone to seek knowledge of it except the One, the Matchless, the Everlasting."'[195]

Therefore, if Allah remains to the Shī'a as the only one who enthrones and dethrones, it follows that Allah did not determine that 'Ali would be the caliph immediately after the Prophet, as he did not get elected. The reason why 'Ali was chosen as the fourth caliph and imam is within the knowledge of Allah (qaḍā' and qadar), which Imam 'Ali himself said is a deep secret outside human knowledge. Therefore, no Shi'ite or Sunni should probe into this secret of Allah's secret any further.

On the Holy Qur'an and Other Shi'ite Holy Books

According to the Shī'a, during the compilation of the Qur'an either in Abu Bakr's or 'Uthmān's period, 'Ali was neither invited to participate in the task nor consulted, even though everyone knew that he had collected the whole Qur'an immediately after the death of the Prophet.[196] The first Shi'ite Hadith compiler, al-Kulaynī, reports the fifth imam, al-Bāqir, as saying, 'Any human being who claims to have collected the Qur'an in its complete form is a liar; only 'Ali b. Abi Ṭālib and the Imams collected it as revealed by Allah.'[197]

The second Shi'ite Hadith compiler, al-Ṣadūq, in his work *I'tiqādāt al-Imāmiyyah*, reports that after Imam 'Ali finished with the compilation of the Qur'an, he said to other *ṣaḥābah*, 'This is the Book of Allah, your Lord, as it was revealed to your Prophet; *not a single word has been added to it or omitted from it.* They said we have no need of it; *we have with us what you possess*' (emphasis added).[198]

Apart from Imam 'Ali confirming that the Qur'an with him was completely the same as the one others possessed, the response of the *ṣaḥābah*, 'We have with us what you possess,' confirms that the Qur'an that was with 'Ali, which the Shī'a are still expecting from the Mahdi, was not different from the Qur'an we possess and follow today. This negates the Hadith of al-Kulaynī mentioned above.

Firstly, if the Qur'an collected throughout the caliphates before 'Ali's was not correct or complete as reported by al-Kulaynī, and if 'Ali kept silent about the book he knew would guide the Muslims of all generations, are the Shī'a not attacking the character of Imam 'Ali, as his actions cannot be accepted by any objective mind as being good? That is – because he had not been invited to compile the Qur'an, but later became the caliph and imam of all Muslims, which provided him with an opportunity to make any amendment (which he did not avail himself of) – he intentionally left every Muslim of every generation to be 'misled' forever. It was convenient and possible for him as caliph to call the attention of all Muslims under him to whatever remained different between the Qur'an in his possession and the original Qur'an compiled by his predecessors.

Secondly, according to the Shī'a, Caliph 'Ali had a voluminous Hadith book dictated to him by the Prophet which contains mentions of what is *ḥalāl* (lawful) and *ḥarām*, (unlawful) and 'everything which the people need'.[199] Imam 'Ali handed over this valuable book only to some of his descendants – not even to all his descendants, let alone his Shī'a or Muslims in general. He also assisted his wife Fāṭimah in writing down all the dictations of the angel Jibrīl's words to her, which collection he also delivered to a small number of his descendants. Since he later received back his 'usurped' right of imamate over all Muslims, what then was the reason for his hiding divine guidance from all of humanity?

No record shows that the Prophet or the Rightly Guided Caliphs before 'Ali ever absconded with such valuable guidance. Ja'far Sobhani confirms that the 'Prophet did not withhold his guidance as regards even the smallest question pertaining to human welfare'.[200] However, according to the Shī'a, Imam 'Ali withheld books containing things pertinent to human welfare, including the naming of what is *ḥalāl* and *ḥarām*. Obviously, Imam 'Ali, in this respect, did not emulate the attitude of the Prophet. If Caliph 'Ali had been cut off by the previous caliphs and was privately training some elites, as the Shī'a claim,[201] was there any Muslim teacher before him who hid the most valuable teaching materials from his students, handing over such a valuable book only to a very small number of his children?

The Shī'a accused the first three caliphs of disallowing the compilation of the Hadith during their caliphates. Imam 'Ali, who compiled his, refused to deliver the resulting book to the whole Muslim world – not even to all his descendants. What is the difference between the lack of compilation (of the first three caliphs) and compilation (of the fourth caliph) without delivering the resulting book to all Muslims?

Besides, why do the Shī'a start their criticism with the first caliph, continuing through to the third one? Why not begin with criticising the Prophet, as the Qur'an was already written down during the Prophet's time? Why don't the Shī'a criticise the Prophet for not compiling his Hadith as done for the Holy Qur'an? Why blame the caliphs for doing what the Prophet did and not doing what the Prophet did not do?

In addition, after Imam 'Ali finished with the Qur'an, why did he leave the Hadiths uncompiled? Why did 'Ali not make amends for this during his caliphate by compiling all of the available Hadths? If there were some compilations during 'Ali's caliphate, where are they, as the Shī'a struggled to determine the authentic Hadiths from the corrupt ones around the time of the Sunni compilations? This is why, like the Sunni, the Shī'a have approved (*ṣaḥīḥ* – authentic) as well as rejected (*ḍa'īf* – weak) Hadiths. Thus, even the Nahj al-Balāghah of Imam 'Ali was later compiled by Abu'l-Ḥasan Muḥammad Ibn al-Ḥusayn al-Radi al-Musawi. All of these things are no more than indirect Shiʿite attacks on the personality of our honourable caliph ʿAli and his previous three brothers for the sole purpose of defending some doctrines.

Furthermore, one of the last sermons of the Prophet (delivered at Ghadīr Khumm), according to the Sunni, includes, 'I have left two things for you which if you follow; you will never go astray, the Qur'an and my Sunnah. The Shiʿah say it is 'the Qur'an and my *Ahl al-bayt*; the two can not separate from each other till the last Day'. Now, all Muslims can still see and have access to both the Qur'an and the Sunnah, as these are the only Islamic texts which, up till now, remain unseparated from each other. The *Ahl al-Bayt,* which the Shīʿa said will remain unseparated, can no longer be contacted or consulted. The last imam, who is still in existence, cannot be consulted even by the Shīʿa, let alone other Muslims. If all the collections of the Hadiths of the imams are what is meant, this confirms the Sunni version of the Prophet's sermon (Qur'an and Sunnah), whether referring to the Sunnah of the Prophet or the imams' Sunnah.

If the Shīʿa still believe that the hidden imam's impact 'is like the sun hidden under the cloud whose impact reflects on the earth', how that hidden imam touches the lives of both Sunni and Shīʿa is not convincingly explained, as the whole Sunni world has not ever felt the impact of the imam in any way.

On Infallibility

Someone must become Shiʿite first before the belief in infallibility can comfortably sit in his or her heart. It is difficult for a non-Shiʿite to believe that Allah ever created any person who never made even a single error or mistake throughout his or her life.

Allah Himself confirms the mistake of Prophet Adam and his wife. Otherwise, what convincing meaning can anyone give to the lamentation of both Adam and Hawa': 'O our Lord! We have wrong our own souls (*ẓalamnā anfusanā*)' (*al-Aʿrāf* 7:21)? Is *ẓulm* not an error, mistake, sin, and/or misdeed? In addition, the same two people confessed that if Allah did not forgive them and have mercy on them, they would definitely be among those who would perish.

Yūnus (Ẓun-nūn) was a confirmed Prophet of Allah according to Sunni and Shī'a alike. He annoyingly left his people without first having the permission of Allah to do so. Was his disobedience to Allah not an error or mistake? He confessed, 'There is no other god except You (Allah), I was in deed *wrong*' (*al-Anbiyā'* 21:87, emphasis added).

The Shī'a aver that the *ṣaḥābah* are not better than all other Muslims. But Allah commands Prophet Muḥammad (pbuh) to declare, 'I am but a *bashar* (human) *like you*' (*al-Kahf* 18:110, emphasis added). Whatever alternative interpretation anyone may suggest, the phrase 'like you' (*mithlukum*) definitely points to other companions, whom the Shi'ites authoritatively declare to be ordinary Muslims and human beings like all of us.[202] The verse therefore means that the difference between the Prophet and his companions, according to the Qur'an and Shi'i understanding of the *ṣaḥābah*, is the aspect of his prophethood and messengership (*yūḥā ilayya*).

The fact that history does not convey the mistakes of some people does not mean they never erred in their entire lives. During an incident regarding 'Āishah, the wife of the Prophet, 'Ali b. Abi Ṭālib was engulfed by the gossip about her, which Allah proved wrong and even recommended that the offenders be punished (Q 24). If the Shi'ite defence is that their own records do not confirm 'Ali as a participant in the gossip, can all the records of the Sunni on this topic be denied? The Shī'a rely on many other Sunni sources which buttress their doctrines regarding many aspects of their religious lives (*fiqh*, history, Hadith, *tafsīr*, etc.). Now, was Imam 'Ali's involvement in gossip not an error on his part? After all, Allah has exonerated the accused.

In any event, the claim of infallibility for all imams is practically irrelevant here, as Imam 'Ali should have known, with his knowledge of everything, hidden or apparent, that Āishah could never have relegated herself to such a debased status. But ʿAli continued to press Āishah's servant for any possible confession. He should have known that his advice to the Prophet to divorce his loving, innocent wife would cost him dearly later with his all-encompassing knowledge of everything. By way of contrast, Usāmah b. Zayd, who was also present with ʿAli and the Prophet in the house of Abu Bakr, was not infallible but bluntly rejected such gossip as nothing but blatant lies about Āishah.

In addition, with the knowledge of everything in the world, Imam ʿAli should have known that going to the Battle of Siffin with disloyal soldiers would cost him dearly. ʿAmr b. ʿĀs, who was not infallible, was full of confidence that his advice to Muʿāwiyah to command his troops to raise copies of the Qur'an would confuse ʿAli's army. With total knowledge of everything, Imam ʿAli should have known all these things even before organising any soldiers for such a terrible war. With total knowledge of everything, Imam ʿAli should have known that the election of the person who would succeed the Prophet would take place at Saqīfah, but he didn't know, as evidenced by his later protest. If he knew, why did he not protect his 'right' instead of protesting? If he did not know, then the claim that total knowledge is endowed to imams is an inaccurate one.

On the matter of Imam Ḥasan b. ʿAli, if the Hadith of *Aṣ-ḥāb al-Kisa* is relevant and reliable, the Prophet included both Ḥasan and Ḥusayn in his supplication to purify all of the descendants. Why did the prayers for infallibility later exclude the descendants of Ḥasan? Why were Ḥasan's descendants not imams? After all, he was the second imam, spiritually and politically speaking, even though he withdrew, whereas Ḥusayn did not rule over any community even for one day, except probably his clan.

The Shīʿa go even further and slash down the family of the Prophet, which the Prophet, like all human beings, would not allow to happen to his family ties. That is, to the Shīʿa, only the chosen imams are the *Ahl al-Bayt*. According to Shomali, 'It is clear that the Prophet had in mind those for whom alone infallibility has been asserted.'[203] That is, infallibility had ben asserted for the thirteen alone: besides the Prophet, the twelve imams and Fāṭimah.

This means that no descendants of Ḥasan are part of the Prophet's family. All the children of Ḥusayn, 'Ali al-Akbar, Ja'far, and 'Abdullāh, who died together with their father in Karbala, were not part of the Prophet's family; the already chosen imam, Ismā'īl of the Ismā'īli Shī'a, who later died before his father, and Imam al-Bāqir's brother, Zayd, who was martyred like Ḥusayn and became imam of the Zaydiyyah, were of another origin. In short, all brothers of the imams born of the same parents but not recognised as imams of the Twelver Shī'a were not part of Prophet's family. This 'assistance' provided to the Prophet to slash down his family for him is unacceptable to the Prophet, his family members, and all human beings of any race or culture.

The Shī'a have continued to criticise the Sunni rulers throughout history. This criticism is no different from what humankind has witnessed from the opposition since time immemorial up to the present day. The opposition party always assumes it is right because it is not in government. Whenever such people assume power, others clearly see their own weakness, as no one is perfect.

It was easy for the Shī'a to formulate their doctrines and to assign infallibility to their imams because none of the imams, except 'Ali, had an opportunity to assume political power. And 'Ali's caliphate or imamate was not perfect, just like the others that are criticised. Imam Ḥasan, who was enthroned by his supporters according to some records, was given a huge sum of money by Mu'āwiyah to withdraw, but authoritative Shi'ite records and some other Sunni records argue that he withdrew not because he collected money from Mu'āwiyah but because Mu'āwiyah succeeded in corrupting Ḥasan's generals.[204] A question to answer is, why would an imam gifted with apparent and hidden knowledge of everything go into war with soldiers already known to be corrupt? As a knower of everything, Imam Ḥasan must have known that his soldiers would be corrupted by Mu'āwiyah, yet he made such futile effort regardless. Can this be accepted as a martyrdom (assuming he died in that war)?

The Shiʿites also defend Imam Ḥasan for relinquishing power to Muʿāwiyah with the agreement that power would return to him after Muʿāwiyah's death.[205] The question is still the same: why would a person who knew of everything in existence, secret and open, be ignorant of what Muʿāwiyah would do to him in favour of his son Yazīd? Imam Ḥasan was supposed to have known this and thereby prevented Muʿāwiyah's ascent to power. Had he known, he probably could have prevented all those alleged misdeeds, misrulings, acts of torture and other un-Islamic actions of the Umayyads.

The Shīʿa should know that many of their imams were kept under strict surveillance by the Umayyad and Abbasid rulers. Some of them had no opportunity, whereas some others were not allowed, to play any major role in governance or perform other public functions, and were condemned to strict private lives. It is easy to claim that such people were infallible since they were not allowed to function publicly so as to have their behaviour assessed by other people.

The fourth imam, Zayn al-ʿĀbidīn, maintained a private lifestyle throughout his life on account of the fact that his family perished at Karbala in his presence. The fifth imam, al-Bāqir, followed the same lifestyle, probably due to the Karbala experience recounted to him by his father. The seventh imam was imprisoned for a long time, first in Basra and later in Baghdad; the tenth imam was imprisoned at Samarra throughout the reign of Caliph al-Muʿtazz; and the eleventh imam (al-ʿAskarī) remained under house arrest nearly all his life,[206] dying at the young age of 27. The ninth imam (al-Jawād) was around 26 years of age when he died. The last imam was not known to the public at all. He disappeared at a very young age.

Thus, given these facts, how is it be possible for any objective mind to accept the assertion that these imams were infallible? The above arguments point to only one fact: perfection belongs only to Allah. As long as the doctrines of any faction were codified by human beings, they will reflect human imperfection. The Ismāʿīli branch of Shīʿa believe that their last imam, Muḥammad b. Ismāʿīl, will come as the Mahdi to reveal all the *imperfections* in the explanations of the six imams previous to their own last imam. This buttresses the acceptance of imperfection of the Imams, by a branch of Shīʿa, even in their divine message.

The Shīʿa also believe that each imam must be the wisest and most knowledgeable of all people during his lifetime. Imam Ḥasan and Imam Ḥusayn, who were also part of the *ṣaḥābah*, were of course knowledgeable, but they did not display any evidence that they were more knowledgeable and more brilliant than many other notable companions. Of course, from both Sunni and Shiʿite records, no one can deny the brilliancy of Imam ʿAli among his contemporaries (the *ṣaḥābah*). Likewise, Imam al-Bāqir and Imam al-Ṣādiq were also brilliant among their contemporaries. These are the only three imams shown in the records to be very brilliant. But this is not to say that any one of them, including Imam ʿAli, was the best among his generation, as the Prophet highly recommended various other *ṣaḥābah*. For instance, according to a Shiʿite authority, ʿAllāmah Tabatabāʾī, quoting from a Sunni record, the Prophet said, 'There is no one between the heaven and earth more truthful than Abu Dhārr' (that is, Abu Dhārr al-Ghiffār).[207] As there is no exception in this recommendation of the Prophet, it means that Abu Dhārr was more truthful than Imam ʿAli, all other imams, and all other human beings.

So, if Abu Dhārr was the most truthful on earth, there is no justification for any Shiʿite to follow Imam ʿAli and his descendants, who were less truthful than Abu Dhārr, as the Prophet's declaration supersedes any other person's. This points to one fact: that the Prophet recommended ʿAli, Abu Dhārr, and numerous other companions does not mean there were no other companions like them, as both Shiʿite and Sunni records are full of such recommendations of various companions.

In the Shīʿas' attempt to defend all their claims, they seek out loopholes to use in their defence. But perfection and infallibility are unique prerogatives of Allah alone which He shares with no other creature.

On Following the Ahl al-Bayt Alone

The Shīʿa believe in following only the twelve imams. It should be noted that only Imam ʿAli, not any other imam, was with the Prophet from the beginning of his mission to the end. Imam Ḥasan and Imam Ḥusayn were still young when the Prophet died. They witnessed only the later parts of his mission. This means that, according to the Shīʿa, out of thousands of the companions who witnessed the mission of the Prophet, only Imam ʿAli's reports about the Prophet, either through him or his descendants, should be trusted and accepted. What of the many sayings, deeds, actions, and reactions of the Prophet in ʿAli's absence? It is not written in any genuine Sunni or Shiʿite record that a companion of the Prophet was with him day and night, without some periods of absence, throughout his mission.

The most convincing practice of any revealed religion is to collect and rely on reports from different disciples or companions of any Prophet, especially those who witnessed the Prophet's mission on various occasions and interacted with him on different levels. If a prophet delivered his revealed book alone without any disciple to record the prophet's deeds and actions, then only his holy book will be followed.

Such is not the case with Islam. In addition to the Holy Qur'an, the last Prophet's deeds, sayings, and actions are part and parcel of Islam, but Imam ʿAli alone was evidently unable to cover or witness all of these deeds, sayings, and actions. It is not acceptable to any objective mind to believe that reports of the last Prophet's deeds and actions over the course of twenty-three years should be restricted to only one companion, when Prophet Muḥammad (pbuh) had thousands of companions. If it is argued that not all those thousands witnessed Muḥammad's missions from the beginning to the end, it would still be permissible to accept these individuals' reports based on what they witnessed after their conversion to Islam, as the Shīʿa accept whatever parts were witnessed by Imam Ḥasan and Imam Ḥusayn.

The Prophet's mission covers many aspects of human endeavours. How could Imam ʿAli's reports alone cover all aspects of the Prophet's life in detail? How can Imam 'Ali's reports on the Prophet's actions in 'Ali's absence be more credible than those of the witnesses to such actions? Is the Shī'a method the correct method to collect credible facts about anyone, either in the past or present?

The Shi'ite Hadith is dominated by reports and verdicts from Imam al-Bāqir and his son al-Ṣādiq. This means that the Shī'a think that reports made about the Prophet from people who were five and six generations removed from him are more credible than those from the *ṣaḥābah* who physically witnessed the events. If the argument against this is that the imams passed their reports from father to son, what is the justification for transferring reports of the Prophet secretly from father to son when the Prophet performed his duties publicly in the company of thousands of his followers?

By analogy, Christianity is as universal as Islam. But the Christians have no descendants of Jesus to explain all the Christ's teachings to them. The Shī'a cannot prove it to the Christians that they do not understand their Religion due to the absence of Christ's descendants to teach his message.

How can anyone be convinced that *ṣalāt*, *zakāt*, *ṣawm*, ḥajj, etc., performed practically in the presence of the last Prophet's companions can only be learnt from either Imam 'Ali alone, or his handful of friends or his descendants? This would mean that other aspects of the Prophet's life can only be described by 'Ali alone. That is, it would mean that other companions did not know how the Prophet used to dress, eat, drink, walk, smile, etc. They could not describe how loving, generous, and accommodating the Prophet was. They could not describe how the Prophet gave judgements or verdicts on different issues in their presence. This is a very difficult belief for the majority of Muslims to accept.

Besides, faithful Muslims are eager to copy the Prophet in all aspects of his life, including matrimonial, domestic, and private aspects. Can reports about the intimacy of the Prophet with his wives be credibly accepted from Imam 'Ali or from the wives themselves? If Imam 'Ali's reports on the private life of the Prophet with his wives contradict the wives' reports, can any sincere Muslim accept those of ʿAli and reject the wives'?

There is no evidence that Imam ʿAli was closer to the Prophet than ʿĀishah was. Of course, both of them were close to the Prophet and educated elites. Given this, what kind of report could Imam ʿAli give about the *taḥajjud* (supererogatory prayers at dawn) of the Prophet which his educated wives like ʿĀishah and Ḥafsah could not give? Now, whether a report is from ʿAli or not, if Imam al-Ṣādiq, who was the sixth descendant of ʿAli, speaks of the *taḥajjud* of the Prophet and contradicts a report made by ʿĀishah, who is to be followed, the wife who slept in the same room with the Prophet for many years or the sixth descendant who never saw a single companion, let alone the Prophet? Unfortunately, it is doubtful that the Shīʿa have a single friend among the educated wives of the Prophet to cite as their basis for reporting the private life of the Prophet.

Of course, Imam ʿAli was married to Fāṭimah, the daughter of the Prophet. Could ʿAli and Fāṭimah better know the private life of the Prophet than his educated wives? The gap of intimacy between a father and daughter is naturally different from the gap between that man and his wives. On top of this, authoritative Shiʿite records confirm that Fāṭimah was unlettered, as her husband used to write everything for her.[208] In addition, Muslims, either Sunni or Shīʿa, do not have many reports from Fāṭimah because she died a few months after the Prophet. Moreover, the whole of the discussions between her and the angel Jibrīl (*Mushaf* Fāṭimah), which could have been useful for both Sunni and Shīʿa, is hidden to everyone.

Regardless of any private training Imam ʿAli received from the Prophet, such information was strictly kept for the consumption of a few family members. And Allah will not question anyone on any instruction that remained undelivered to humanity.

In order to put an end to complicating issues between the remaining two factions of Muslims, the Shīʿa should accept their loopholes like the Sunni do, and both should move on towards proper conciliation.

Conclusion: Sunni-Shi'ite Relationship - Conciliation or Complication?

'In its original form, the Sunni–Shiite dispute was not concerned with the fundamentals of religion.... Over time, it has degenerated from a quarrel about the Prophet's successorship into a ritual, theological, and legal rift which, at least obliquely, affects certain basic beliefs and attitudes... The polemics are clearly of two kinds: those dealing with historical personalities, especially some of the crucial figures of early Islam, and those dealing with concepts and doctrines. The Shiites are usually concerned with personalities, and the Sunnis are usually concerned with concepts and doctrines.'[209]

Even though the early Muslims made efforts to reunite the followers of the last Prophet after the *fitnah* (trouble of riots, divisions and wars) broke out during the periods of rule of the third and fourth caliphs, those efforts never succeeded for long. The unification of various sects under one umbrella of the *Ahl al-Sunnah wa'l-Jamā'ah* only survived for some time. The disunity within the Sunni world today, with a seemingly uncountable number of subsects, is pathetic and disheartening. More important than this, the chaos, conflict, and hatred between the Sunni and the Shī'a, superlative in degree, is a serious problem. A religion revealed for the purpose of uniting humanity has been turned by its adherents into a religion of disunity. Efforts to reconcile Islam's adherents always end up bringing more conflicts or complications.

On the Sunni–Shi'ite relationship, various leaders and scholars have made several efforts at reconciliation which have ended up as either being short-lived unity or morphing into armed conflicts. This is because the initial problems that gave rise to the conflicts, namely politics and tribalism (the latter now being nationalism), coupled with other selfish interests, have today become part and parcel of Muslim belief. The political problem continues to date in its original form, and tribalism long ago extended to become nationalism. That is, the artificial geographical boundaries have finally shattered the efforts of all Muslims trying to preach the unity for which Islam stands. An additional factor, something which is the most stubborn barrier to unity, is the intolerance among a portion of Muslims in both Sunni and Shiʿite factions. Efforts have been made by some leaders and scholars for conciliation, but these are always thwarted by other leaders and scholars from both sides.

For instance, on the part of Shīʿa, as early as the time of Muḥammad Nurbakhsh (d.1464 CE), a descendant of the Shiʿite seventh imam, Mūsā al-Kāzim, tried to reinterpret some Shiʿite doctrines in order to reconcile his faction with the Sunni. Yet, his efforts died shortly after his own death. Another Shiʿite monarch, Nadir Shah, the founder of the Afsharid State in Iran in 1743, prohibited the vilification and repudiation of the first three caliphs, at least publicly. He also took steps to persuade the Sunni to recognise Shiʿism as an additional school of thought (*madh-hab*), which efforts Shiʿite scholars rejected. Part of the reason for the Shīʿa rejection of Nadir Shah's efforts was that they disliked the idea that their imams, especially those who codified the Shīʿa doctrines (e.g. Imam Jaʿfar al-Ṣādiq and his father, Imam al-Bāqir), would then be equal to the Sunni founders of *madh-habs*, whereas the Shīʿa considered their imams to be above the Sunni founders, by far, considering their infallible status. Besides, the doctrine of Shiʿism crumbles if it is seen as just a *madh-hab* under the Sunni Schools of jurisprudence. The efforts ended when Nadir Shah was assassinated in 1747 CE.[210] Nadir's effort led to the organisation of a congress between the Sunni and Shiʿite Islamic scholars in Najaf, but this was a failure.[211]

On the part of the Sunni at the political level, one of the Ottoman sultans, Abdul Hamid II, tried to reconcile with the Shiʿite Persian Empire. The two sects fought alongside the Turkish army in a *jihād* against the British. This secured the support of some Sunni scholars, who started to preach for unity of all Muslims and made efforts to reconcile the Sunni with the Shīʿa. These scholars, among others, included Jamāl al-Din al-Afghāni al-Asadabadi, Muḥammad Abduh, Rashīd Riḍa, and Kawākibi. According to Sabrina Mervin:

> Jamal al-Din's idea was simple. The inability of Muslims to unite had precipitated the decline of the two great empires and facilitated European incursions into Islamic lands. The torn body of the 'Umma had to be put back together to

> form a common front against the invasions, smoothing over doctrinal divergences and uniting in political action. A union was the remedy for all ills.[212]

The efforts of these scholars and political leaders did not succeed on account of the creation of the present Middle Eastern states, with each citizen becoming more loyal to his or her new state. Tribalism expanded to become nationalism, even though showing loyalty to one's tribe at the expense of Islam is still actively practised in many Arab lands. All throughout history, 'the life of the Arabs was dominated by tribal loyalty, with members of a tribe seeing their own lives as bound up with that of their chief'.[213]

Nonetheless, in 1931, a congress of Sunni and Shīʿa was held in Jerusalem. A Shiʿite scholar, Sheikh Muḥammad Ḥusayn Kashif al-Ghitāʾ of Iraq, delivered a sermon in Masjid al-Aqṣa 'calling for unity in facing the assaults of the West and for the defense of Palestine'.[214]

These reconciliatory efforts continued to yield dialogues between a few leading Shiʿite and Sunni *ʿulamāʾ* (scholars), such as al-Zanjāni, Muḥammad Khalisi, and Muḥammad Ḥusayn al-Ghitāʾ (Shiʿite scholars), and al-Azhari rectors such as al-Marāghī and Maḥmūd Shaltūt (Sunni scholars). These friendly communications continued throughout the 1930s and 1940s. Then, between 1947 and 1948, an Iranian Shiʿite scholar, Muḥammad Taqi Qummi, in conjunction with al-Azhar *ʿulamā* and Egyptian politicians, established *Jamāʿat* or *Dār al-Taqrīb al-Madhāhib* (Organisation for Rapprochement Between Schools of Thought).[215] This organisation published a review, '*Risālat al-Islāmiyyah*' ('The Message of Islam'), as an avenue for cordial Sunni–Shiʿite discussions. The organisation also created a forum where, according to Sheikh Shaltūt, as quoted by Hamid Enayat, 'The Ḥanafi, the Māliki, the Shāfiʾi and the Ḥambali sit next to the Imāmi and Zaydi round one table discussing literary accomplishments, Sufism and Jurisprudence, in an atmosphere pervaded by spirits of fraternity, a sense of affection, love and comradeship.'[216]

Because of this friendly atmosphere, al-Azhar University Rector Sheikh Maḥmūd Shaltūt, in February 1959, officially issued a *fatwah* (verdict) authorising Shiʿi *fiqh* (jurisprudence) to become part of the curriculum of this great University. This put Shiʿite jurisprudence on the same level with the four Sunni schools of thought. The study of Shiʿi *fiqh* had probably not been taught at al-Azhar, either for the past nine hundred years since its establishment in 361 AH/972 CE,[217] or at least, since the conquest of Egypt by Ṣalāḥ al-Dīn al-Ayūbi around 1170s CE.

As these efforts were rapidly moving towards success, just like the previous ones had been, another political *fitnah* still set in. Retaliating against Iran for its recognition of Israel, Egypt broke its diplomatic relationship with Iran in 1960, which affected every effort made by scholars and politicians for reconciliation.

However, instead of resulting in total disunity, this step of the Iranian government led to wider cooperation, as around 150 *ʿulamā'* from various parts of the world issued a *fatwa* calling for the entire international Muslim community to create 'an attitude of *jihād* against the Shah of Iran for his pro-Israeli policy'.[218]

Three years later, Muslims witnessed the dissolution of unity, as internal revolution started in Iran against the Shah, led by Ayatollah Ruḥullah Khomeini, strongly assisted by Gamal Abdel Nasser and his Arab nationalist campaign against the Shah, which 'called into being, united front between Iranian Shiʿism and Arab Sunnism',[219] coupled with over 150 scholars' *fatwa* against the Shah's government. This led to the success and existence of the present Islamic Republic of Iran.

It is unfortunate that instead of Muslims learning from the success brought about by their unity, especially their success in the Iranian Revolution, they revived their old enmity when sectarian sentiments and other thoughts set in internally and externally in Iran after the revolution, as well as in other Arab lands. Lack of tolerance on both sides increased to the extent that the Shīʿa and Sunni waged war against each other in different forms: the war of Arab Sunnism and Persian Shiʿism, the war of the Arab nationalism of Iraq, and the Persian nationalism of Iran (i.e. the Iran–Iraq War of the 1980s).

Today, the situation is an Arab Sunni and Arab Shi'ite war based on mere differences in their understanding of the same Islam. This has given rise to the Saudi-led Sunni war against the Iranian-led Shī'a (e.g. the Saudi-led coalition against the Houthis of Yemen). Wherever any people of either faction live as the minority, they live as second-class citizens in their homeland. For instance, the Sunnis in Iran (those in Kurdistan and Baluchistan) and the Shī'a in Saudi Arabia (those in Najran, the Nakhawila in Madīnah, and those in the eastern region). The same or an even worse situation applies in other Muslim countries that turn terrorists and suicide bombers against one another despite the condemnations of terrorism[220] by Allah and the Prophet.

The *fitnah* created on account of the political interest of those inside the circle of notable personalities among the early Muslims has today engulfed uncountable individuals across the world; the *fitnah* created by tribal sentiments between very few Arab tribes and clans has resulted in the current endless shedding of blood and subsequent loss of innocent lives across continents. Abu'l-'Aliyya al-Riyāhi, mentioned by Ibn Sa'd in his *Tabaqāt al-Kabīr*, was a witness to the initial conflict. This was his decision and conclusion, as revealed by Aisha Bewley:

> In the time of the conflict between 'Ali and Mu'āwiyah, I was young and eager and preferred to fight ... so, I made excellent provision in order to join the army. At Siffin, the ends of the two armies could not be seen because each side was so large. If one side were destroyed the other side would be destroyed as well. I thought to myself, 'Which of the two groups will I consider to be unbelievers? Which will I consider to be believers? Who can force me to take part in this?' I continued to reflect on it until I went back and left them.[221]

This is the lamentation of a witness to the original conflict over a thousand years ago. It means, on the one hand, that ignorance of the original conflict affects contemporary Muslims on both sides. The following is the opinion of Imam Khomeini: 'The Muslim people must become acquainted with the fundamental ordinances of Islam. Ignorance exists on both sides, among Sunnis and Shiʿis alike, and it is as a result of this ignorance that clashes and enmity have arisen.'[222]

On the other hand, the selfish interests of some Muslim leaders and religious scholars, especially their love of wealth, power, and other worldly things, or their hypocritical motives, are what have furthered the course of the conflict. No doubt, natural differences among human beings, as well as the allegorical nature of some Qur'anic verses, leads to the creation of diverse opinions or groups, but this alone does not automatically lead to hatred, with tolerance and free-mindedness preached by Islam. According to Nathan C. Funk and Abdul Aziz:

> Conflict occurs when individuals or groups are unable to discipline or sublimate passion (*hawa*) or egotism through adherence to ethical and legal standards. Subservience to internal craving and external fixation alienates human beings from their true purpose, leading to antagonism, conflict, and oppression. Where there is competitive pursuit of wealth, glory, and the granting of greater priority to tribalism (*ʿaṣabiyya*) and selfish desires than to revealed values and norms, humans have failed to grasp their proper status and role within the scheme of reality.[223]

Allah knows, as His Apostle knew, that opinions will divide Muslims. That is why both the Qur'an and the Sunnah continuously emphasise unity through humility and tolerance of one another, exhorting Muslims not to be divided through hatred into sects. If sincere Islam is being preached and followed by leaders and scholars, according to Ahmad Zaki Hammad, regardless of the reasons that led to their diverse opinions, 'the differences themselves should not be looked upon as being inherently evil; on the contrary, they can be great help in learning as well as guarding us from the unyielding rigidity that has stunted the growth and contribution of Muslim Ummah in recent times.'[224]

Today, many Sunnis are convinced that the Shīʿa codified many false doctrines as part of Islam, which, to some, disqualify Shiʿism from being a legitimate part of Islam. To such Sunnis, the Shīʿa turn 'Ali and his descendants into superhumans, and they worship as heroes the select imams among them, thwarting their appointment to the divine and condemning the pious three caliphs in the process.

The Shīʿa are also convinced that the Sunnis, as the true majority, are on the erring path because their three caliphs usurped the right of the Prophet's candidate and tampered with Islamic rituals and laws without any authority given them to do so by Allah and His Apostle. The Shīʿa alledge that the Sunni follow the caliphs and the companions who were not divinely appointed to be obeyed, downplay the orders of the Prophet, and do not believe in the divinity of the imams. All these things, to some Shiʿites, cause the Sunnis to be, at the least, unfaithful, hypocritical Muslims, and at the most, unbelievers.

According to Haamid Enayat, So long as the proponents of both factions treat the prejudices they inherited from previous generations, and their personal interpretations of religion, as revealed or divine truths, there will be no prospect of reconciliation.[225] So long as Muslims refuse to yield to Allah's instruction, they will see a continuation of internal insecurity, external threat, and the constant shedding of Muslim blood, because they have 'split up their religion, and become sects, each faction is rejoicing in what it has' (*al-Rūm* 30:32).

> And hold fast, all of you, by the Rope (Islam) which Allah (stretches out for you) and be not divided among your selves; and remember with gratitude Allah's favour on you; for you were enemies and He joined your hearts in love, so that by His grace, you (all) become brothers (of the same faith) *Āl-Imrān* 3:103
>
> Indeed, those who have divided their religion and become sects, you (Prophet), are not with them in anything (of such). Their affair is only (left) to Allah; then He will inform them the truth of all they used to do. (*al-Anʿām* 6:159)
>
> And obey Allah and His Messenger; and fall into no disputes, lest you lose courage and (then) your strength (or power)

> departs; and be patient (with one another): For Allah is with the patient ones. (*al-Anfāl* 8:46)

So long as what Muslims consider to be true Islam is closely intertwined with sectarian *ʿaqīdahs* and various racial idiosyncrasies (Shiʿism with Persian culture and Iranian ideology, Sunnism with Saudi politics and Arab clan patriotism, and either of these combined with Indo-Pakistan peculiarities, Kurdish identity, African heritage, and/or Western interference), any hope of unity is unrealistic.

The Prophet warned Muslims of all generations before his departure:

> O people, lend me an attentive ear, for I know not whether after this year I shall ever be among you again, nor ever address you again from this spot. Therefore, listen to what I am saying carefully and take these words to those who could not be present here today. O people, just as you regard this month, this day and this city as sacred, so too, regard the life and property of every Muslim as sacred trust. ... Hurt no one so that no one will hurt you too. Remember that you will certainly meet your Lord, and will definitely reckon your deeds. ... Beware of Shayṭān, for the safety of your Religion. He has lost all hope that he will ever be able to lead you astray in big things, so beware of following him in small things. ... Beware! Do not go astray after I am gone. O People, listen to me attentively! ... All mankind is from Ādam and Hawāʾ [Eve]. ... Know that every Muslim is a brother to every Muslim, and all Muslims constitute a single brotherhood. Therefore, remain united and be not divided. ... Be my witness O Allah that I have delivered Your Message to Your people.[226]

Notes

Chapter 1: The Sunnis

1 Robert Caspar, *A Historical Introduction to Islamic Theology: Muhammad and the Classical Period* (Rome: Pontificio Instituto di Studi Arabi e d'Islamica, 1998), 212.

2 William Montgomery Watt, *The Formative Period of Islamic Thought* (Oxford: Oneworld Publications, 2002), 256.

3 M. M. A'zami, *Studies in Hadith Methodology and Literature* (Indianapolis: American Trust Publications, 1413 AH/1992 CE), 49.

4 Ahmad Amīn, *Fajr al-Islam*, 10th edn (Cairo: Maktabah al-Nahḍat al-Miṣriyyah, 1965), 212.

5 Muhammad Muhsin Khan, 'Introduction', in *Sahih al-Bukhari – Arabic–English*, i (New Delhi: Kitab Bhavan, 1987), xvi.

6 A'zami, *Studies in Early Hadith Literature*, 301–2.

7 Alfred Guillaume, *Islam* (Middlesex: Penguin Books, 1964), 91.

8 Mohammad Hashim Kamali, *Principles of Islamic Jurisprudence* (Cambridge: Islamic Text Society, 1991), 65.

9 Muhammad Zubayr Ṣiddīqī, *Hadith Literature: Its Origin, Development and Special Features*, ed. Abdal Hakim Murad (Cambridge: Islamic Text Society, 1993), 31–2. Ṣiddīqī cites examples of forgeries during the Prophet's period and Abu Bakr's period. Abu Bakr and 'Umar were very strict in accepting Hadiths from people because some were forged. Of course, there were a few instances of the Prophet exiling some companions who tried to alter some verses of the Qur'an, let alone the Hadith.

10 Guillaume, *Islam*, 91.

11 Abu Ameenah Bilal Philips, *The Evolution of Fiqh (Islamic Law and the Madhhabs)* (Riyadh: Tawheed Publications, 1411 AH/1990 CE), 47–8.

12 These include, among many others, (1) *al-Ṣaḥīḥ* (sound); (2) *al-Ḥasan* (fair); (3) *al-Ḍa'īf* (weak); (4) *al-Mawḍū'* (forged); (5) *al-Mu'allal* (defective); (6) *al-Afrād* (isolated); (7) *al-Munkar* (unfamiliar); (8) *al-Mu'aḍal* (problematic); (9) *al-Musnad* (supported); and (10) *al-Muttasil* (uninterrupted). See Ibn al-Ṣalāḥ

al-Shahrazūrī, *An Introduction to the Science of Ḥadīth - Kitāb Maʿrifat anwāʿ ʿIlm al-Ḥadīth*, ed. Eerik Dickinson (Reading: Garnet Publishing Limited and Centre for Muslim Contribution to Civilization, 2006), 2–3.

13 al-Khalil Ibn ʿAbdullāh al-Khalili, *al-Irshād fī maʿrifat ʿUlamāʾ al-Ḥadīth*, ed. ʿĀmir Ahmad Haydar (Makkah: Dār al-Fikr, 1993), 6.

14 M. A. O. Abdul, *The Selected Traditions of al-Nawawi: Arabic Text, Transliteration and Commentary* (Lagos: Islamic Publications Bureau, n.d.), 12.

15 Aʿzami, 72. *See also* Abdur-Rahman I. Doi, *Sharīʿah: The Islamic Law* (London: Ta-Ha Publishers, 1984), 55.

16 Scott C. Lucas, *Constructive Critics, Hadith Literature and the Articulation of Sunni Islam: The Legacy of the Generation of Ibn Saʿd, Ibn Maʿin and Ibn Hambal* (Leiden: Brill, 2004). See chapters 1 and 2 for detailed discussions on this.

17 The collections of the following scholars were not ranked like those in the first category. This does not mean that authentic Hadiths are not found among them. (1) Aḥmad b. Ḥanbal, (2) Abū Dāwūd al-Ṭayālīsī, (3) ʿUbayd Allāh b. Mūsā, (4) Is-ḥāq b. Rāhawayh, (5) Humayd al-Kishshi (or al-Kashshi), (6) ʿAbdullāh b. ʿAbd al-Raḥmān al-Dārimī, (7) Abu Yaʿlā al-Mawsilī, (8) al-Ḥasan b. Ṣufyān, (9) Abu Bakr al-Bazzār, (10) Sufyān b. ʿUyayna, (11) Sufyān al-Thawrī, (12) Abu'l Qāsim Sulaymān al-Ṭabarānī, (13) Abu Bakr Aḥmad al-Bayḥaqī, (14) Abu al-Ḥasan ʿAli al-Dāraquṭnī, (15) Abu ʿUthmān Saʿīd b. Manṣūr. *See* Muhammad Zubayr Ṣiddīqī, *Hadith Literature*, 70–2; *see also* Ibn al-Ṣalāḥ al-Shahrazūrī, *An Introduction to the Science of Ḥadīth*, 21–2.

18 Ibn al-Ṣalāḥ al-Shahrazūrī, *An Introduction to the Science of Ḥadīth*, 22.

19 Ṣiddīqī, *Hadith Literature*, 73.

20 Renowned scholars among his students include Ikrimah, Saʿīd b. Jubayr; Mujāhid b. Jabr; and ʿAṭāʾ b. Abi Rabāḥ. See Abu Ameenah Bilal Philips, *Uṣool at-Tafseer: The Methodology of Qur'anic Explanation* (Sharjah: Dār al-Fatah, 1997), 19.

21 Later competent scholars among Ubayy's students include Zubayr b. Aslam; Abu al-ʿĀliyah; and Muḥammad b. Kaʿb al-Quradhī. *See* Philips, *Uṣool at-Tafseer*, 19.

22 They include ʿAlqamah b. Qays; al-Aswad b. Yazīd; ʿĀmir al-Shaʿbi; and Ḥasan al-Baṣri. *See* Philips, *Uṣool at-Tafseer*, 15.

23 Philips, *Uṣool at-Tafseer*, 15.

24 A. Yusuf Ali, 'Commentaries on the Qur'an', in *The Holy Qur'an: Text, Translation and Commentary* (Leicester: Islamic Foundation, 1975), ix.

25 Ibid. ix.

26 Ahmad Von Denffer, *ʿUlūm al-Qur'ān: An Introduction to the Science of the Qur'an* (Leicester: The Islamic Foundation, 1989), 125. *See* Doi, *Sharīʿah: The Islamic Law*, 35.

27 Khurshid Ahmad, 'Foreword', in Sayyid Abdul Aʿala Mawdudi, *Towards Understanding the Qur'an*, i, ed. and tr. Zafar Ishaq Ansari (Leicester: The Islamic Foundation, 1408 AH/1988 CE), ix.

[28] Watt, *The Formative Period*, 262.

[29] Kristina Nelson, *The Art of Reciting the Qur'an* (Austin: University of Texas Press, 1985), 14.

[30] Ibid. 14.

[31] These *ṣaḥābah* include (1) 'Abdullāh b. Mas'ūd, (2) Ubayy b. Ka'b, (3) 'Ali b. Abi Ṭālib, (4) 'Abdullāh b. 'Abbās, (5) Abu Mūsā al-Ash'ari, (6) 'Umar al-Khaṭṭāb, (7) Anas b. Mālik, (8) Zayd b. Thābit, (9) 'Abdullāh b. 'Amr, (10) 'Ubayd b. 'Umar, (11) Ibn al-Zubayr, (12) Sālim, (13) Abu Bakr al-Ṣiddīq, (14) 'Uthmān b. 'Affān, (15) Abu Darda, (16) Mu'ādh b. Jabal, (17) Abu Ayūb Anṣārī, (18) 'Ubāda b. al-Ṣāmit, (19) Tamīm Dārī, (20) 'Āishah bint Abi Bakr, (21) Ḥafṣah bint 'Umar, and (22) Umm Salamah.

[32] Philips, *Uṣool at-Tafseer*, 175.

[33] The four *ṣaḥābah* were Zayd b. Thābit; 'Abdullāh b. al-Zubayr; Sa'īd b. al-'Ās; and 'Abd al-Raḥmān b. Ḥārith b. Hishām.

[34] Von Denffer, *'Ulūm al-Qur'ān*, 53.

[35] Philips, *Uṣool at-Tafseer*, 155. Some scholars say that the number of copies produced during Caliph 'Uthmān's time was more than seven.

[36] Yasin Dutton, *The Origin of Islamic Law: The Qur'an, the Muwaṭṭa' and Madinan 'Amal* (Surrey: Curzon Press, 1999), 56.

[37] Philips, *Uṣool at-Tafseer*, 170.

[38] Ibid. 171–2.

[39] Von Denffer, 119–20.

[40] Ibid. 119.

[41] Ibid. 63.

[42] University of Birmingham, *The Birmingham Qur'an Manuscript* (Birmingham: University of Birmingham, 2015), 6.
The discovery of the four pages of the early Qur'an was announced on 22 July, but the pages were exhibited between 2 and 25 October 2015. The present author visited the exhibition at the Bramall Music Building of the University of Birmingham on 8 October and compared the verses with the present ones. The authenticity of what we have today is perfectly confirmed with the early divine documents. According to the University of Birmingham (in the United Kingdom), the manuscripts have been kept in their Cadbury Research Library since 1930s. They had been transported from the Middle East to Birmingham by a researcher, Alphonse Mingana (d.1937), together with many other documents. These had been originally catalogued as part of the eighth- or ninth-century manuscripts. The documents were taken to Oxford University's Radiocarbon Accelerator Unit to test the goatskin or sheepskin containing the verses. The result of that test dates the parchments to the seventh century with 95.4 per cent probability. In addition, with careful study of similar manuscripts in other places, the University of Birmingham

proposed that the four pages in Birmingham are part of the sixteen pages presently kept at Bibliothèque Nationale de France in Paris. The sixteen pages' origin was linked to 'Amr b. al-'Ās Mosque in Fustat, the ancient Islamic capital of Egypt. *See* University of Birmingham, *The Birmingham Qur'an Manuscript*, 8–9.

However, during the conflicts between 'Ali and Mu'āwiyah – that is the Battle of Siffin – 'Amr b. al-'Ās suggested that pages of Qur'anic parchment be raised up so as to confuse 'Ali's army.The tactic really worked for them. This action of 'Amr b. al-'Ās prevented Caliph 'Ali from conquering Mu'āwiyah's army. Mu'āwiyah subsequently rewarded 'Amr b. al-'Ās with the governorship of Egypt, the capital of which was Fustat. Those pages of the Qur'an distributed to the army probably were not put together as a single entity. Some of them might have submitted their copies, while others may have kept theirs. The Mosque of 'Amr b. al-'Ās, where the Paris copies came from, was built in 642 CE. The Birmingham copies might have been bought, along with other documents from individuals who inherited them from their ancestors, by Alphonse Mingana in the early 1930s. In any case, the authenticity of the Qur'an remains intact to date.

43 Muhammad Abu Zahra, *The Four Imams: Their Lives, Works and Their Schools of Thought*, tr. Aisha Bewley (London: Dar al-Taqwah, 2001), 299.

44 Kamali, *Principles of Islamic Jurisprudence*, 1–2.

45 Philips, *The Evolution of Fiqh*, 42.

46 Majid Khadduri, 'The Historical Background of the Risāla', in Muhammad Ibn Idrīs al-Shāfi'i, *al-Risālat fī Uṣūl al-Fiqh*, tr. Majid Khadduri (Cambridge: The Islamic Text Society, 2003), 5.

47 Ahmad Hasan, *Analogical Reasoning in Islamic Jurisprudence: A Study of the Juridical Principles of Qiyās* (Islamabad: Islamic Research Institute, 1986), 6.

48 Abu Zahra, *The Four Imams*, 184–5.

49 Mohammad Muslehuddin, *Islamic Jurisprudence and the Rule of Necessity and Need* (Jeddah: Abdul Qasim Book Store, 1410 AH), 29–30.

50 Philips, *The Evolution of Fiqh*, 58.

51 Sayyid Sābiq, *Fiqh Sunnah*, tr. Muhammad Sa'eed Dabas and Jamal al-Din M. Zarabozo (Indianapolis:American Trust Publications, n.d.), xii.

52 Abu Zahra, 301.

53 Sābiq, *Fiqh Sunnah*, xi–xii.

54 Abu Zahra, 24.

55 Philips, *The Evolution of Fiqh*, 48.

56 Abu Zahra, 185.

57 Philips, *The Evolution of Fiqh*, 53.

58 Watt, 268.

59 Kamali, 4.

60 Khadduri, 'The Historical Background of the Risāla', 42–3.

61 Ṣiddīqī, *Hadith Literature*, 112–13.

62 Muhammad ibn Idrīs al-Shāfi'i, *al-Risāla fī Uṣūl al-Fiqh*, tr. Majid Khadduri (Cambridge: The Islamic Text Society, 2003), 180.

63 Imran Ahsan Khan Nyazee, *Theories of Islamic Law* (Islamabad: Islamic Research Institute, 1945), 179.

64 Other founders of Sunni *madhhabs* (schools of jurisprudence) include Imams Abd al-Raḥmān b. al-Awzā'ī, Dāwūd b. 'Ali al-Ẓāhirī, Muḥammad b. Jarīr al-Ṭabarī, Sufyān al-Thawrī, and al-Layth b. Sa'īd.

65 Khadduri, 42–3.

66 Abdul Hakim I. Matroudi, *The Hambali School of Law and Ibn Taymiyyah: Conflict or Conciliation* (London and New York: Routledge, Taylor & Francis Group, 2006), 7–8.

67 D. Sourdel, 'The Abbasid Caliphate', in P. M. Holt, Ann K. S. Lambton, and Bernard Lewis (eds.), *The Cambridge History of Islam* (Cambridge: Cambridge University, 1970), 124–5.

68 Watt, 253.

69 The Islamic scholars intended permanent prohibition, but the prohibition didn't last beyod a number of centuries, as some contemporary scholars are making efforts to revive Mu'tazilism.

70 Abu Zahra, 23. Of course, Shi'ite scholars attest to the fact that 'Ali and his wife, Fāṭimah, "sought aid from the companions" after Abu Bakr was elected. In fact, Sayyid Mujtaba Musavi Lari devotes pages 41 – 46 of his book to how 'Ali used to 'fight' for his imamate right and reasons for his continuous endurance till he was finally elected. *See* Sayyid Mujtaba Musavi Lari, *Imamate and Leadership: Lessons on Islamic Doctrines (Book Four)*, tr. Hamid Algar (Qum, Iran: Foundation of Islamic Cultural Propagation in the World, 1417/1996), 41- 46.

71 Ibid. 456. Shūra members were the most respected of the remaining companions (mentioned in the text in the parentheses). The group was constituted by the second caliph, 'Umar b. al-Kaṭṭāb, to produce the next caliph among themselves. They finally produced Caliph 'Uthmān, the third caliph.Their full names are: 'Uthmān b. 'Affān; 'Ali b. Abi Ṭālib; Sa'd b. Abi Waqqās; Abdul-Raḥmān b. Awf; Zubayr b. 'Awwām and Ṭalḥah b. 'Ubayd Allāh.

72 Ibid. 23.

73 Watt, 266.

74 Ibid.

75 al-Haj Maulana Fazul-ul-Karim, *Imam Ghazali's Ihya Ulum-id-Din – Book 1* (Lahore: Sind Sagar Academy, 1971), 142–3. *See also* Abu'l-Hasan 'Ali b. Ismā'īl al-Ash'arī, *al-Ibānah 'an Uṣūl ad-Diyānah – Elucidation of Islam's Foundation*, tr. Walter C. Klein (New Haven: American Oriental Society, 1940), 33.

76 Fazul-ul-Karim, *Imam Ghazali's Ihya Ulum-id-Din*, 143.

[77] 'Abdul-Karīm al-Shahrastāni, *The Summa Philosophiae of al-Shahrāstani: Kitāb Nihāyatu 'l-Iqdām fī 'ilmi 'l-kalām*, tr. and ed. Alfred Guillaume (Oxford: Oxford University Press, and London: Humphrey Milford, 1934), 151, no. 478.

[78] Fazul-ul-Karim, 143.

[79] Zahra, 456.

[80] *Kalām* is dialectic theology, the science of applying one's reason or intellect to teach or explain one's views or beliefs and defend such opinions concerning Islam's six articles of faith and other related topics, as well as the political legitimacy of fellow Muslims of the same or an opposing faction. In dialectic theology, the focus at first is always on the capability of using one's reason or intellect (*'aql*) in dialectical arguments with a view to winning over an opponent and/or defending one's beliefs or doctrines from any attack or condemnation. In this science, the existence of an opponent is very important, because the aim is not just merely to choose an argument but rather to win over an opponent and rationally and convincingly defend one's beliefs as to be acceptable to members of one's group, opposing groups, and neutral groups. *See* Abdul Ganiy O. Oloruntele, *Introduction to Islamic Theology: The Historical Origin and Doctrines of the Early Muslim Sects* (Ilorin: Taofiqullah Publishing House, 1422 AH/2001 CE), 8–9.

[81] al-Shahrastāni, *The Summa Philosophiae*, 148, no. 469.

[82] Ibid. no. 470.

[83] al-Ash'ari, *al-Ibānah 'an Uṣūl ad-Diyānah*, 33, 52.

[84] Adam R. Gaiser, 'What Do We Learn About the Early Kharijites and Ibādiyya from Their Coins?', in *Journal of the American Oriental Society*, 30, 2 (April–June 2010): 167.

[85] Watt, 264.

[86] Ibid.

[87] Ignaz Goldziher, *Introduction to Islamic Theology and Law*, tr. Andras and Ruth Hamori (Princeton: Princeton University Press, 1981), 161.

[88] Watt, 264.

[89] Scott C. Lucas, *Constructive Critics*, 371.

[90] Watt, 268–71.

[91] Ibid. 268.

[92] Abu al-Hasan 'Ali b. Ismā'il al-Ash'ari, *Kitāb Maqālāt al-Islāmiyyīn wa Ikhtilāf al-Muṣallīn* (Istanbul: Maṭba'at Dawala, 1929), 3.

[93] Ibid. 5.

[94] Watt, 267.

Chapter 2: The Shīʿa

1. Marshall G. S. Hodgson, 'How Did the Early Shiʿa Become Sectarian?', in Etan Kohlberg (ed.), *The Formation of the Classical Islamic World – Shi'ism*, xxxiii, pp. 1–13 (Hant (Great Britain) and Burlington (USA): Ashgate Publishing Company, 2003), 1.
2. William Montgomery Watt, *The Formative Period of Islamic Thought* (Oxford: Oneworld Publications, 2002), 57.
3. Ayatollah Jaʿfar Sobhani, *Doctrines of Shiʿi Islam: A Compendium of Imami Beliefs and Practices*, tr. and ed. Reza Shah-Kazemi (London and New York: I. B. Tauris Publishers, in association with the Institute of Ismaili Studies, 2001), 97.
4. Ibid. article 83.
5. Arzina R. Lalani, *Early Shīʿī Thought: The Teachings of Imam Muḥammad al-Bāqir* (London and New York: I. B. Tauris, in association with the Institute of Islamaili Studies, 2000), 2.
6. Syed Amir Ali, *The Spirit of Islam: A History of the Evolution and Ideals of Islam with a Life of the Prophet* (London: Chatto and Windus, 1974), 294.
7. Heinz Halm, *Shiʿa Islam – From Religion to Revolution*, tr. Allison Brown (Princeton: Markus Wiener Publishers, 1999), 21.
8. A. Rahim, *Islamic History* (Lagos: Islamic Publication Bureau, 1981), 123.
9. Ibid.
10. Ali, *The Spirit of Islam*, 303.
11. Philip K. Hitti, *History of the Arabs* (London: Macmillan Publishers, 1970), 440.
12. Halm, *Shiʿa Islam*, 17.
13. Watt, *The Formative Period*, 41.
14. Lalani, *Early Shīʿī Thought*, 7.
15. Halm, *Shiʿa Islam*, 21.
16. Karim Douglas Crow, 'The Death of al-Husain b. ʿAli and Early Shi'i View of the Imamate', in Etan Kohlberg (ed.), pp. 41–116, *The Formation of the Classical Islamic World*, 43.
17. Hodgson, 'How Did the Early Shiʿa Become Sectarian?', 3.
18. Muhammad Husayn Tabatabāʾī, *Shi'ite Islam*, tr. and ed. Seyyed Hossein Nasr (London: George Allen & Unwin Ltd, 1975), 60–1.
19. Andrew J. Newman, *The Formative Period of the Twelver Shiʿism – Hadith as Discourse Between Qum and Baghdad* (Surrey: Corzon Press, 2000), 6.
20. Aṣ-Ṣadūq Muhammad b. ʿAli b. Bābawayh, *Risālah al-Iʿtiqādāt al-Imāmiyyah: A Shi'ite Creed*, tr. Asif A. A. Fyzee (London: Oxford University Press and Islamic Research Association, 1942), 102. *See also* S. Waheed Akhtar, *Early Shiʿite Imamiyyah Thinkers* (New Delhi: Ashish Publishing House, 1988), xxxii–xxxiii.
21. Crow, 'The Death of al-Husain b. ʿAli', 54.
22. Hitti, *History of the Arabs*, 447.

[23] Moojan Moomen, *An Introduction to Shi'i Islam: The History and Doctrines of Twelver Shi'ism* (New Haven and London: Yale University Press, 1985), xiii.

[24] Halm, *Shi'a Islam*, 21.

[25] Khawla Bint Ja'far was among the captives when the people of Yamāmah disregarded the payment of zakat and war was declared on them. The people of Yamāmah recognised the woman in Madīnah and appealed on her behalf of Imam 'Ali to spare the honour of her family the blemish of slavery. She was freed and married by Caliph 'Ali. *See* 'Ali Ibn Abi Ṭālib, *Nahj al-Balāgha: Sermons, Letters and Sayings - Arabic & English*, compiled by As-Sayyid Abu'l-Hasan Muhammad Ibn al-Husayn ar-Radi al-Musawi, tr. Syed Ali Raza, i, (Qum: Ansariyan Publications, 1971), 88.

[26] Heinz Halm, *Shi'ism*, tr. Janet Watson and Marian Hill (Edinburgh: Edinburgh University Press, 2004), 16.

[27] Ibid. 17.

[28] Ibid.

[29] Lalani, 34.

[30] Ibid.

[31] Ibid.

[32] Halm, *Shi'ism*, 17–18.

[33] Ibid. 19.

[34] Ibid. *See also* Newman, *The Formative Period of the Twelver Shi'ism*, 6.

[35] Akhtar, *Early Shi'ite Imamiyyah Thinkers*, xxxiii.

[36] Etan Kohlberg, 'Early Shi'ism in History and Research', in Etan Kohlberg (ed.), *The Formation of the Classical Islamic World*, p. xx. *See also* Abu al-Hasan 'Ali b. Ismā'il al-Ash'ari, *Kitāb Maqālāt al-Islāmiyyīn wa Ikhtilāf al-Muṣallīn* (Istanbul: Maṭba'at Dawala, 1929), 65.

[37] Farhad Daftary, *A Short History of the Ismailis* (Edinburgh: Edinburgh University Press, 1998), 29.

[38] Ibid.

[39] Ibid. 32.

[40] Halm, *Shi'ism*, 28.

[41] Akhtar, xxxiii.

[42] Daftary, *A Short History of the Ismailis*, 51. *See also* Farhad Daftary, *The Ismailis: Their History and Doctrines* (Cambridge: Cambridge University Press, 1995), 37.

[43] Daftary, *A Short History*, 51.

[44] Farhad Daftary, *A Short History*, 52; and Daftary, *The Ismailis*, 137.

[45] Daftary, *A Short History*, 53; and Daftary, *The Ismailis*, 139.

[46] Tabatabā'ī, *Shi'ite Islam*, 79.

[47] Daftary, *A Short History*, 53–4, and Daftary, *The Ismailis*, 140.

[48] Daftary, *A Short History*, 55–6, and Daftary, *The Ismailis*, 141.

[49] Daftary, *A Short History*, 56, and Daftary, *The Ismailis*, 141.

50 Daftary, *A Short History*, 56, and Daftary, *The Ismailis*, 142.
51 Halm, *Shi'ism*, 167.
52 Ibid. 160.
53 Abu Ja'far Muḥammad b. Ya'qūb b. Is-ḥāq al-Kulaynī, *al-Uṣūl min al-Kāfī*, i (Tehran: Maktabat al-Ṣadūq, 1281 AH), 59.
54 Tabatabā'ī, 82.
55 Lutfullah al-Ṣāfī, *Ma'al Khatīb fī Khutūtihi al-Arīḍah* (Tehran: n.p., 1987), 62–3. *See also* Bābawayh, *Risālah al-I'tiqādāt al-Imāmiyyah*, 85.
56 Tabatabā'ī, 49.
57 al-Kulaynī, *al-Uṣūl min al-Kāfī*, i, 228.
58 al-Kulaynī, *al-Uṣūl min al-Kāfī*, ii (Tehran: Maktabat al-Ṣadūq, 1281 AH), 633.
59 Ibid. 634.
60 Bābawayh, *Risālah al-I'tiqādāt al-Imāmiyyah*, 86–7.
61 al-Kulaynī, *al-Uṣūl min al-Kāfī*, i, 240–1.
62 Ibid. 242.
63 Ibid. 239–40.
64 Sobhani, *Doctrines of Shi'i Islam*, 178–9, article 137.
65 Ibid. *See also* al-Kulaynī, *al-Uṣūl min al-Kāfī*, i, 239.
66 Sobhani, 93.
67 Ibid.
68 Seyyed Hossein Nasr, 'Introduction', in Muhammad Husayn Tabatabā'i, *A Shi'ite Anthology*, tr. William C. Chittick (London: Muhammadi Trust of Great Britain and Northern Ireland, 1980), 5.
69 Ibid. 6.
70 Sobhani, 177, article137.
71 Tabatabā'ī, 94.
72 Sobhani, 176, article 136.
73 Tabatabā'ī, 49.
74 Ibid.
75 Sobhani, 179, article 137.
76 Ibid.
77 William C. Chittick, 'Introduction', in Muhammad Husayn Tabatabā'i, *A Shi'ite Anthology*, tr. William C. Chittick (London: Muhammadi Trust of Great Britain and Northern Ireland, 1980), 16; Yann Richard, *Shi'ite Islam: Polity, Ideology and Creed*, tr. Antonia Nevill (Oxford (UK) and Cambridge (USA): Blackwell Publishers, 1995), 7; Sobhani, *Doctrines of Shi'i Islam*, 181, article 138. *See also* Moojan Moomen, *An Introduction to Shi'i Islam*, 174. Ja'far Sobhani mentions some Hadith transmitters, together with their Hadith, as weak and untrustworthy. These include Aḥmad b. Muḥammad Ṣayyārī and 'Ali b. Aḥmad al-Kūfī. *See* Ayatollah Ja'far Sobhani, *Doctrines of Shi'i Islam*, 94, article 82.
78 Richard, *Shi'ite Islam*, 7.

79 Tabatabā'ī, 173.

80 Mohammed A. Shomali, *Shi'i Islam: Origins, Faith and Practices* (London: Islamic College for Advanced Studies Press, 2003).

81 Akhtar, xxii.

82 Ibid. xv.

83 Shomali, *Shi'i Islam*, 18, quoting from Ibn Asākir, ii, 442.

84 Ibid. quoting from al-Suyūtī, *al-Durr al-Mathūr*, viii, 589.

85 Ibid. 21, quoting from Ibn Kathīr, *al-Bidāyah wa al-Nihāyah*, vii, 369.

86 Sheikh al-Mufīd, *Kitāb al-Irshād: The Book of Guidance into the Lives of the Twelve Imams*, tr. I. K. A. Howard (Sussex and London: Balagh Books and the Muhammadi Trust of Great Britain and Northern Ireland, 1981), 30–1. *See also* Sobhani, *Doctrines of Shi'i Islam*, 102, article 86, quoting from Ibn Hanbal, *Musnad*, i, 159; Aṭ-Ṭabarī, *Tārīkh al-Rusul wa al-Mulūk* (Beirut: n.p., 1408 AH/1986 CE), ii, 406; and al-Ṭabarī, *Jāmi'al-Bayān* (Beirut: n.p., 1980), xix, 74–5 (commentary on *Sūrah al-Shu'rā'*).

87 Sayyid Athar Abbas Rizvi, *A Socio-Intellectual History of the Ithna-'Asharī Shī'īs in India*, i (Campbell, Australia: Ma'rifa Publishing House, 1986), 18. *See also* Sobhani, *Doctrines of Shi'i Islam*, 105, article 87; and Sheikh al-Mufīd, *Kitāb al-Irshād*, 124.

88 Sobhani, 100, article 85.

89 The Shi'a refer to the Sunni records, including that of Ibn Jarīr Ṭabri, *Tārīkh al-Ṭabarī*, ii, 436; Ismā'īl ibn 'Umar Ibn Kathīr, *al-Bidāyah wa al-Nihāyah*, v (Beirut: Dār al-Kutub al-'Ilmīyah, 1994), 227; and Ibn Abi al-Ḥadīd, *Sharh Nahj al-Balāghah*, i (Tehran: Wizārat al-Thaqāfah wa-al-Irshād al-Islāmī, al-Dā'irah al-'Āmmah lil-Nashr wa-al-I'lām, 1988), 133.

90 Tabatabā'ī, 69 n. 11.

91 Shomali, 93.

92 Tabatabā'ī, 212.

93 Shomali, 94.

94 Ibid. 95.

95 Kohlberg, 'Early Shi'ism in History and Research', xvi.

96 Sobhani, 111, article 92.

97 Ibid. 110, article 91.

98 Ibid. 111, article 92.

99 Tabatabā'ī, 187.

100 Abdul Karim al-Shahrastāni, *The Summa Philosophiae of al-Shahrastāni-Kitāb Nihāyatu'l – Iqdām fi 'ilmi'l-Kalām*, tr. and ed. Alfred Guillaume (Oxford: Oxford University Press, and London: Humphrey Milford, 1934), 153, no. 484.

101 Sobhani, 111–12, article 92. To the Sunnis, that verse (33:33) is unambiguously addressing the wives of the Prophet generally. It means that the Ahl al-Bayt here definitely include all his wives. However, the Shī'a, at times, include a companion

of the Prophet, Salmān al-Fārisī, as a member of the *Ahl al-Bayt*. See Sobhani, 'Glossary', in *Doctrines of Shi'i Islam*, 222.

[102] Matti Moosa, *Extremist Shiites: The Ghulat Sects* (Syracuse: Syracuse University Press, 1988), 77. In addition to Shi'ite sources, he refers to Sahih Muslim, iv, Hadith 5955.

[103] Shomali, 105.

[104] Sobhani, 112, article 92.

[105] Kohlberg, 'Early Shi'ism in History and Research', xvii.

[106] Sobhani, 179, article 137.

[107] Ja'far Subhani, *The Message*, tr. Islamic Seminary (Tehran: Foreign Department of Be'that Foundation, 1984), 750.

[108] Bābawayh, *Risālah al-I'tiqādāt al-Imāmiyyah*, 96–7.

[109] Halm, *Shi'a Islam*, 30.

[110] Ibid. 137.

[111] Ibid. 31.

[112] Crow, 54.

[113] Halm, *Shi'ism*, 137.

[114] Ibid.

[115] Ibid.

[116] Ibid. 138. *See also* Moomen, 182.

[117] Ayoub, *Redemptive Suffering in Islam: A Study of the Devotional Aspects of 'Āshūrā in the Twelver Shi'ism* (Hague, Paris, New York: Mouton Publishers, 1978), 184. Ayoub quotes the Hadith of Sheikh as-Ṣadūq, p. 235.

[118] Ayoub, *Redemptive Suffering in Islam*, 185–6, quoting the Hadith of Ibn Qawlawayh, p, 112.

[119] Halm, *Shi'a Islam*, 26.

[120] Richard, 11.

[121] Ibid. 8–9.

[122] Ayoub, *Redemptive Suffering*, 191, quoting the Hadith of Ibn Bābawayh, *Man lā Yaḥḍuruhū al-Faqīh*, ed. I. K. A. Howard, in *Al Serat*, 2, 2 (1976): 359–60.

[123] Moosa, *Extremist Shiites*, xvi.

[124] Halm, *Shi'a Islam*, 63.

[125] Tabatabā'ī, 232–3.

[126] Ibn Kathīr, *The Life of the Prophet Muhammad: al-Sīra al-Nabawiyya*, iv, tr. Trevor Le Gassick (Reading: Garnet Publishing and the Centre for Muslim Contribution to Civilization, 2000), 347. *See also* Mahmoud M. Ayoub, *The Crisis of Muslim History: Religion and Politics in Early Islam* (Oxford: Oneworld Publications, 2003), 12.

[127] Halm, *Shi'a Islam*, 28.

[128] Ibid. 29.

[129] Tabatabā'ī, 209–10.

[130] Crow, 46–7.

[131] Tabatabā'ī, 210. *See also* Moojan Moomen, *An Introduction to Shi'i Islam*, 165.

[132] Tabatabā'ī, 210–11. *See also* Moomen, 163.

[133] Moomen, 164.

[134] Sobhani, 119, article 101.

[135] Tabatabā'ī, 214.

[136] Ibid.

[137] Sheikh al-Mufīd, 524.

[138] Haamid Enayat, 'Shi'ism and Sunnism', in Seyyed Hossein Nasr, Hamid Dabash, and Seyyed Vali Reza Nasr (eds.), pp. 64–83, *Shi'sm: Doctrines, Thoughts and Spirituality* (Albany: State University of New York Press, 1988), 75.

[139] Sobhani, 117, article 97.

[140] Halm, *Shi'a Islam*, 34.

[141] Moomen, 167.

[142] Sheikh al-Mufīd, 541–54. *See also* Moomen, 168–70.

[143] Subhani, *The Message*, 758–9.

[144] Ibid. 764; and Tabatabā'ī, 69 n. 11.

[145] Subhani, 765–6.

[146] Ibid. 766.

[147] Subhani quotes various Sunni records to buttress his points, namely (1) Ṣaḥīḥ al-Bukhāri, Kitāb al-'ilm, i, 22, and ii, 14; (2) Ṣaḥīḥ Muslim, ii, 14; (3) Musnad Aḥmad, i, 325; (4) Ibn Sa'd', Ṭabaqāt al-Kubra, ii, 244; (5) and Ibn Abi al-Ḥadīd, Sharḥ Nahj al-Balāghah, ii, 29.

[148] Subhani, 769.

[149] Tabatabā'ī, 41.

[150] Ibid.

[151] Ṭālib, *Nahj al-Balāgha: Sermons, Letters and Sayings*, 50–1.

[152] Tabatabā'ī, 49.

[153] Enayat, 'Shi 'ism and Sunnism', 71–2.

[154] Tabatabā'ī, 183.

[155] Enayat, 72–3; *See also* Ṭālib, 67; and Tabatabā'ī, 48.

[156] al-Kulaynī, *al-Uṣūl min al-Kāfī*, i, 195.

[157] Enayat, 77.

[158] al-Kulaynī, *al-Uṣūl min al-Kāfī*, ii, 217.

[159] Tabatabā'ī, 223.

[160] Saeed Ismaeel, *The Difference between the Shi'ah and the Majority of the Muslim Scholars* (Riyadh: World Assembly of Muslim Youths, 1988), 21, quoting from a Shi'ite magazine, *al-Ḥukūmat al-Islāmiyyah*.

[161] Tabatabā'ī, 224.

[162] Ibid.

[163] Sobhani, 152, article 124.

[164] Ibid. 154, article 125.
[165] Mohammad Sharif, *Innocently Accused* (Karachi: Islamic Seminary Publications, 1979), 14.
[166] Ibid.
[167] Sayyid Muhammad Rizvi, *Marriage and Morals in Islam* (Winnipeg: Islamic Education Foundation, 1990), 74–5.
[168] The Shī'a quote from Ṣaḥīḥ al-Bukhāri, Hadith 53, in the chapter on nikāḥ; Ṣaḥīḥ Muslim, Hadith nos. 3243–8.
[169] The Sunni scholars include Ibn Rushd (Bidāyat al-Mujtahidah, ii, 58); Imam Fakhr Rāzi Shāfi' (*Tafsīr al-Kabīr*, iii, 200); Imam al-Nawawi (Ṣaḥīḥ Muslim, ix, 181); Imam Baiḍāwi Shāfi' (*Tafsīr*, i, 259): and Ibn Kathīr al-Dimashqi (*Tafsīr*, i, 474).
[170] Sharif, *Innocently Accused*, 16.
[171] Tabatabā'ī, 227.
[172] Ibid.
[173] Sobhani, 191, article 144; *also* Tabatabā'ī, 231.
[174] Sobhani, 189, article 144, quoting from Muhammad Hasan Ḥurr 'Āmili, *Wasā'l al-Shi'ah*, iii, Chapter 4, narration 1.
[175] Sobhani, 189, article 144, quoting from *Wasā'il al-Shi'ah*, iii, Chapter 4, narration 4.
[176] Sobhani, 190, article 144, quoting from Sahih Muslim, ii, 151, chapter on 'Joining together of two prayers while at home'.
[177] Sobhani, 190, quoting from 'Commentary of al-Zarqāni on al-Muwaṭṭa' of Imam Mālik on joining together of the two prayers while at home and on a journey'.
[178] Sobhani, 191, article 144.
[179] Sobhani, 185–6, article 142.
[180] Moomen, 178; and Richard, 8.
[181] Tabatabā'ī, 46.
[182] The Sunni sources quoted include *Sunan Abu Dāwūd*, i, 196, Hadith nos. 730 and 736.
[183] Tabatabā'ī, 46.
[184] Richard, 8. The present author also witnessed Sh'iite Muslims prostrating on such a clay tablet on different occasions in the United Kingdom.
[185] Tabatabā'ī, 231.
[186] Sobhani, 195, article 147.
[187] Tabatabā'ī, 232.
[188] Sobhani, 107 article 89; and Tabatabā'ī, 181.
[189] Imam Khomeini, *Islam and Revolution: Writings and Declarations*, tr. Hamid Algar (London, Melbourne, and Henley: KPI, 1981), 43.
[190] Tabatabā'ī, 182.
[191] Ibid. 192.

[192] Muhammad Husain Hykal, *The Life of Muhammad*, tr. Ismā'īl Rāgī al-Fārūqī (Indianapolis: American Trust Publications, 1993), 329.

[193] Muhammad Ibn Sa'd, *Kitāb Tabaqāt al-Kabir*, tr. Moinul Haq (Karachi: Pakistan Historical Society, 1972), 303.

[194] Wilferd Madelung, *The Succession to Muhammad: A Study of the Early Caliphate* (Cambridge: Cambridge University Press, 2004), 17.

[195] Bābawayh, *Risālah al-I'tiqādāt al-Imāmiyyah*, 36–7.

[196] Tabatabā'ī, 49.

[197] al-Kulaynī, *al-Uṣūl min al-Kāfī*, i, 228.

[198] Bābawayh, *Risālah al-I'tiqādāt al-Imāmiyyah*, 87.

[199] Sobhani, 179, article 137.

[200] Sobhani, 100, article 84.

[201] Tabatabā'ī, 50.

[202] Ibid. 94.

[203] Shomali, *Shi'i Islam*, 57.

[204] Ibid. 56; and Tabatabā'ī, 195. 'Mu'awiyah gradually subverted the generals and commanders of Imam Hasan's army by paying them large sums of money and making them deceiving promises, until the army rebelled against Imam Hasan' (Tabatabā'ī, 195).

[205] Ibid. 'Finally, the Imām was forced to make peace and to yield the caliphate to Mu'awiyah, provided it would again return to Imam Hasan after Mu'awiyah's death and the Imam's household and partisans would be protected in every way' (Tabatabā'ī, 195).

[206] Newman, *The Formative Period of the Twelver Shi'ism*, 6.

[207] Tabatabā'ī, 52, quoting from Ibn Mājah.

[208] al-Kulaynī, *al-Uṣūl min al-Kāfī*, i, 240, narration 2.

[209] Enayat, 71.

[210] Ibid. 78.

[211] Sabrina Mervin, 'On Sunnite–Shi'ite Doctrinal and Contemporary Geopolitical Tensions', in Brigitte Maréchall and Sami Zemni, eds., pp. 11–24, *The Dynamics of Sunni–Shia Relation: Doctrine, Transnationalism, Intellectuals and the Media* (London: Hurst & Company, 2013), 16.

[212] Ibid. 17.

[213] Sobhani, 101, article 85.

[214] Mervin, 'On Sunnite–Shi'ite Doctrinal and Contemporary Geopolitical Tensions', 17.

[215] Ibid.; and Enayat, 82.

[216] Enayat, 82.

[217] Ibid. 81.

[218] Ibid. 82.

[219] Ibid.

220 **On terrorism**: There are various meanings and usages of the word *terrorism*, but today terrorism erroneously attributed to Muslims alone. However, as long as a few Muslims engage in terrorist acts, it is necessary to remind them of Allah's warnings:

> Indeed, those who subject the believing men and women to (any form of) tribulation and do not repent, for them is the punishment of hell, and for them is a burning torment.(*al-Burūj* 85:10)

> Whoever kills a person (Muslim or not, unjustly), except as a punishment for murder or for disorder in the land, it is as if he has killed all of humanity. (. *al-Mā'idah* 5:32)

Also, the Prophet says, 'Indeed, Allah shall inflict His punishment upon those who torture people in the life of this world.' *See* Abdul Hamid Siddiqi, *Sahih Muslim*, tr. English (New Delhi: Kitab Bhavan, 2000), in the Book of Piety, Filial Duty, and Good Manners.

On suicide bombing, the Qur'an says, 'And do not cast your selves into destruction with your own hands – and adopt righteousness. Verily, Allah loves the righteous' (*al-Baqarah* 2:195).

Also, the Prophet says, 'Whoever commits suicide with something will be punished with same thing in the Hell-Fire.' *See* Muhammad Muhsin Khan, *The Translation of the Meaning of Sahih al-Bukhari, Arabic–English*, viii (New Delhi: Kitab Bhavan, 1978), 81; and *Kitāb al-Adab – The Book of Good Manners*, Hadith no. 126.

> It is narrated on the authority of Abu Hurayra that the Messenger of Allah observed: He who killed himself with steel [weapon] would be the eternal denizen of the Fire of Hell and he would have that weapon in his hand and would be thrusting that in his stomach forever and ever; he who drank poison and killed himself would sip that in the Fire of Hell where he is doomed forever and ever; and he who killed himself by falling from [the top of] a mountain would constantly fall in the Fire of Hell and would live there forever and ever.
>
> (See Sahih Muslim, i, 74, Hadith no. 199, in the Book of Īmān, the chapter titled 'Suicide is the gravest sin'.)

The excerpt from Hadith 126 means that whosoever kills himself through suicide bombing will continuously bomb himself in Hell with hellfire bombs forever and ever.

Muhammad Tahir-ul-Qadri devotes pages 221–37 of his book to legal rulings of numerous notable Imams on terrorism and suicide bombings. All the imams

(Abū Ḥanīfah, Mālik, Shāfiʿī, Ibn Hanbal, Sufyān al-Thawri, Ibn Qudāmah, al-Mawardi, al-Nawawi, al-Sarakhsi, al-Kāsāni, al-Marghīnāni, et al.) strictly condemn terrorism of any kind. Therefore, Tahir-ul-Qadri concludes thus: 'Human life is neither owned nor acquired; it is a gift and trust from God. The blessing of life serves as a basis for all other blessings. It is for this reason that Islam direct people to safeguard their lives and forbids suicide'. *See* Muhammad Tahir-ul-Qdri, *Fatwah on Terrorism and Suicide Bombings* (London: Minhaj-ul-Qur'an International, 2010), 78.

221 Aisha Bewley, 'Introduction', in Muḥammad Ibn Saʿd, *The Men of Medinat*, vi, tr. Aisha Bewley (London: Ta-Ha Publishers, 1418 AH/1997 CE), viii.

222 Khomeini, *Islam and Revolution*, 326.

223 Nathan C. Funk and Abdul Aziz Said, *Islam and Peacemaking in the Middle East* (Boulder and London: Lynne Reinner Publishers, 2009), 149.

224 Ahmad Zaki Hammad, 'Reviewer's Note', in Sayyid Sābiq, *Fiqh Sunnah*, trans. Muhammed Saʿeed Dabas and Jamal al-Din M. Zarabozo (Indianapolis: American Trust Publications, n.d.), xvii.

225 Enayat, 78.

226 For the full text of the Prophet's address, see Ismāʿīl Ibn Kathīr, *al-Bidāyah wal-Nihāyah*, i (Beirut: Maktabah al-Maʿārif, n.d.), 109–202. *See also* Adil Salahi, *Muhammad, Man and Prophet* (Leicester, UK; Nairobi, Kenya; and Kano, Nigeria: The Islamic Foundation, 1423 AH/2002 CE), 784–6; and Muhammad Husayn Hykal, *The Life of Muḥammad*, tr. Ismāʿīl Rāgī A. al-Fārūqī (Indianapolis: American Trust Publications, 1993), 486–7.

References

Abdul, M. A. O., *The Selected Traditions of al-Nawawi: Arabic Text, Transliteration and Commentary* (Lagos: Islamic Publications Bureau, n.d.).

Abu Zahra, Muhammad, *The Four Imams: Their Lives, Works, and Their Schools of Thought*, tr. Aisha Bewley (London: Dar al-Taqwah, 2001).

Ahmad, Khurshid, 'Foreword', in Sayyid Abdul A'ala Mawdudi, *Towards Understanding the Qur'an*, i, tr. and ed. Zafar Ishaq Ansari (Leicester: The Islamic Foundation, 1408 AH/1988 CE).

Akhtar, S. Waheed, *Early Shi'ite Imamiyyah Thinkers* (New Delhi: Ashish Publishing House, 1988).

Ali, A. Yusuf, *The Holy Qur'an: Text, Translation and Commentary* (Leicester: Islamic Foundation, 1975).

Ali, Syed Amir, *The Spirit of Islam: A History of the Evolution and Ideals of Islam with a Life of the Prophet* (London: Chitto and Windus, 1974).

al-Ash'ari, Abu'l-Hasan 'Ali b. Ismā'il, *Kitāb Maqālāt al-Islāmiyyīn wa Ikhtilāf al-Muṣṣallīn* (Istanbul: Maṭba'at Dawla, 1929).

——— *al-Ibānah 'an Uṣūl ad-Diyānah: Elucidation of Islam's Foundation*, tr. Walter C. Klein (New Haven: American Oriental Society, 1940).

Amīn, Ahmad, *Fajr al-Islam*, (10th edn, Cairo: Maktabah al-Naḍah al-Miṣriyyah, 1965).

Ayoub, Mahmoud, M, *The Crisis of Muslim History: Religion and Politics in Early Islam* (Oxford: Oneworld Publications, 2005).

——— *Redemptive Suffering in Islam: A Study of the Devotional Aspects of 'Āshūrā in the Twelver Shi'ism* (Hague, Paris, and New York: Mouton Publishers, 1978).

A'zami, M.M., *Studies in Early Hadith Literature* (Indianapolis: American Trust Publications, 1978).

---------- *Studies in Hadith Methodology and Literature* (Indianapolis: American Trust Publications, 1413 AH/1992 CE).

Bewley, Aisha, 'Introduction', in Muhammad Ibn Sa'd, *The Men of Medinat*, i, tr. Aisha Bewley (London: Ta-Ha Publishers, 1418 AH/1997 CE).

Caspar, Robert, *A Historical Introduction to Islamic Theology: Muhammad and the Classical Period* (Rome: Pontificio Instituto di Studi Arabi e d'Islamica, 1998).

Chittick, William C., 'Introduction', in Muhammad Husayn Tabatabā'i, *A Shi'ite Anthology*, tr. William C. Chittick (London: Muhammadi Trust of Great Britain and Northern Ireland, 1980).

Crow, Karim Douglas, 'The Death of al-Husain b. 'Ali and Early Shi'i View of the Imamate', in Etan Kohlberg (ed.), *The Formation of the Classical Islamic World - Shi'ism*, xxxiii (Hant (Great Britain) and Burlington (USA): Ashgate Publishing Company, 2003), 41–116.

Daftary, Farhad, *A Short History of the Ismailis* (Edinburgh: Edinburgh University Press, 1998).

——— *The Ismailis: Their History and Doctrines* (Cambridge: Cambridge University Press, 1995).

Denfer, Ahmad Von, *'Ulūm al-Qur'ān: An Introduction to the Science of the Qur'ān* (Leicester: The Islamic Foundation, 1989).

Doi, 'Abdur-Raḥmān I., *Sharī'ah: The Islamic Law* (London: Ta-Ha Publishers, 1984).

Dutton, Yasin, *The Origin of Islamic Law: The Qur'an, the Muwaṭṭa' and Madinan 'Amal* (Surrey: Curzon Press, 1999).

Enayat, Haamid, 'Shi'ism and Sunnism', in Seyyed Hossein Nasr, Hamid Dabashi, and Seyyed Vali Reza Nasr (eds.), *Shi'sm: Doctrines, Thoughts and Spirituality* (Albany: State University of New York Press, 1988), 64–83.

Fazul-ul-Karim, al-Haj Maulana, *Imam Ghazali's Ihya Ulum-id-Din – Book 1* (Lahore: Sind Sagar Academy, 1971).

Funk, Nathan C., and Said, Abdul Aziz, *Islam and Peacemaking in the Middle East* (Boulder and London: Lynne Reinner Publishers, 2009).

Gaiser, Adam R., 'What Do We Learn About the Early Kharijites and 'Ibādiyya from Their Coins?', *Journal of the American Oriental Society*, 130, 2 (April–June 2010): 167.

Goldziher, Ignaz, *Introduction to Islamic Theology and Law*, tr. Andras and Ruth Hamori (Princeton: Princeton University Press, 1981).

Guillaume, Alfred, *Islam*, (Middlesex: Penguin Books, 1964).

Halm, Heinz, *Shi'a Islam – From Religion to Revolution*, tr. Allison Brown, (Princeton: Markus Wiener Publishers, 1999).

——— *Shi'ism*, tr. Janet Watson and Marian Hill (Edinburgh: Edinburgh University Press, 2004).

Hasan, Ahmad, *Analogical Reasoning in Islamic Jurisprudence: A Study of the Juridical Principles of Qiyās* (Islamabad: Islamic Research Institute, 1986).

Hitti, Philip K., *History of the Arabs* (Hong Kong: Macmillan Publishers, 1970).

Hodgson, Marshall G. S., 'How Did the Early Shi'a Become Sectarian?', in Etan Kohlberg (ed.), *The Formation of the Classical Islamic World: Shi'ism*, xxxiii (Hant (Great Britain) and Burlington (USA): Ashgate Publishing Company, 2003).

Hykal, Muhammad Husain, *The Life of Muhammad*, tr. Ismā'īl Rāgī al-Fārūq (Indianapolis: American Trust Publications, 1993).

Ibn Abi Ṭālib, 'Ali, *Nahj al-Balāgha: Sermons, Letters and Sayings – Arabic and English*, compiled by as-Sayyid Abu'l-Hasan Muhammad Ibn al-Husayn ar-Radi al-Musawi, tr. Syed Ali Raza, i (Qum: Ansariyan Publications, 1971).

Ibn Bābawayh, al-Ṣadūq Muḥammad b. 'Ali, *Risālah al-I'tiqādāt al-Imāmiyyah: A Shi'ite Creed*, tr. Asif A. A. Fyzee (London: Oxford University Press and Islamic Research Association, 1942).

Ibn Kathīr, *The Life of the Prophet Muhammad: al-Sīra al-Nabawiyya*, iv, tr. Trevor Le Gassick (Reading: Garnet Publishing and the Centre for Muslim Contribution to Civilization, 2000).

Ibn Sa'd, Muhammad, *Kitāb Tabaqāt al-Kabir*, tr. Moinul Haq (Karachi: Pakistan Historical Society, 1972).

Ismaeel, Saeed, *The Difference between the Shi'ah and the Majority of the Muslim Scholars* (Riyadh: World Assembly of Muslim Youths, 1988).

Kamali, Mohammad Hashim, *Principles of Islamic Jurisprudence* (Cambridge: Islamic Text Society, 1991).

Khadduri, Majid, 'The Historical Background of the Risāla', in Muhammad Ibn Idrīs al-Shāfi'i, *al-Risāla fī Uṣūl al-Fiqh*, tr. Majid Khadduri (Cambridge: The Islamic Text Society, 2003).

al-Khalīl Ibn 'Abdullāh al-Khalili, *al-Irshād fī ma'rifat 'Ulamā' al-Ḥadīth*, ed. 'Āmir Aḥmad Haydar (Makkah: Dār al-Fikr, 1993).

Khan, Muhammad Muhsin, *Sahih al-Bukhari - Arabic–English* (New Delhi: Kitab Bhavan, 1987).

Khomeini, Imam, *Islam and Revolution: Writings and Declarations*, tr. Hamid Algar (London, Melbourne, and Henley: KPI, 1981).

Kohlberg, Etan, 'Early Shi'ism in History and Research', in *The Formation of Classical Islamic World - Shi'ism*, Etan Kohlberg (ed.), xxxiii (Hant (Great Britain) and Burlington (USA): Ashgate Publishing Company, 2003).

al-Kulaynī, Abu Ja'far Muhammad b. Ya'qūb b. Is-ḥāq, *al-Uṣūl min al-Kāfī*, i (Tehran: Maktabah as-Ṣadūq, 1281 AH).

Lalani, Arzina R., *Early Shī'ī Thought: The Teaching of Imam Muḥammad al-Bāqir* (London and New York: I. B. Tauris, in association with the Institute of Islamaili Studies, 2000).

Lari, Sayyid Mujtaba Musavi, *Imamate and Leadership: Lessons on Islamic Doctrines (Book Four)*, tr. Hamid Algar (Qum, Iran: Foundation of Islamic Cultural Propagation in the World, 1417/1996).

Lucas, Scott C., *Constructive Critics, Hadith Literature and the Articulation of Sunni Islam: The Legacy of the Generation of Ibn Sa'd, Ibn Ma'in and Ibn Hanbal* (Leiden: Brill, 2004).

Madelung, Wilferd, *The Succession to Muhammad: A Study of the Early Caliphate* (Cambridge: Cambridge University Press, 2004).

Matroudi, Abdul Hakim I., *The Hanbali School of Law and Ibn Taymiyyah: Conflict or Conciliation* (London and New York: Routledge, Taylor & Francis Group, 2006).

Mervin, Sabrina, 'On Sunnite–Shi'ite Doctrinal and Contemporary Geopolitical Tensions', in Brigitte Maréchall and Sami Zemni (eds.), *The Dynamics of Sunni–Shia Relation: Doctrine, Transnationalism, Intellectuals and the Media* (London: Hurst & Company, 2013), 11–24.

Moojan Moomen, *An Introduction to Shi'i Islam: The History and Doctrines of Twelver Shi'ism* (New Haven and London: Yale University Press, 1985).

Moosa, Matti, *Extremist Shiites: The Ghulat Sects* (Syracuse: Syracuse University Press, 1988).

al-Mufīd, Sheikh, *Kitāb al-Irshād: The Book of Guidance into the Lives of the Twelve Imams*, tr. I. K. A. Howard (Sussex and London: Balagh Books and the Muhammadi Trust of Great Britain and Northern Ireland, 1981).

al-Musawi, Sayyid Hashim, *Minhajul-Fiqhu'l Islami: A Course in Islamic Jurisprudence* (London: Department of Translation and Publication, the Islamic Culture and Relations Organisation, 1417 AH/1997 CE).

Muslehuddin, Mohammad, *Islamic Jurisprudence and the Rule of Necessity and Need* (Jeddah: Abu'l Qasim Book Store, 1410 AH).

Nasr, Seyyed Hossein, 'Introduction', in Muhammad Husayn Tabatabā'I (ed.), *A Shi'ite Anthology*, tr. William C. Chittick (London: Muhammadi Trust of Great Britain and Northern Ireland, 1980).

Nelson, Kristina, *The Art of Reciting the Qur'an* (Austin: University of Texas Press, 1985).

Newman, Andrew J., *The Formative Period of the Twelver Shi'ism – Hadith as Discourse Between Qum and Baghdad* (Surrey: Corzon Press, 2000).

Nyazee, Imran Ahsan Khan, *Theories of Islamic Law* (Islamabad: Islamic Research Institute, 1945).

Oloruntele, Abdul Ganiy O., *Introduction to Islamic Theology: The Historical Origin and Doctrines of the Early Muslim Sects* (Ilorin: Taofiqullah Publishing House, 1422 AH/2001 CE).

Philips, Abu Ameenah Bilal, *Uṣool at-Tafseer: The Methodology of Quranic Explanation* (Sharjah: Dār al-Fatah, 1997).

——— *The Evolution of Fiqh (Islamic Law and the Madh-habs)* (Riyadh: Tawheed Publications, 1411 AH/1990 CE).

Rahim, A., *Islamic History* (Lagos: Islamic Publications Bureau, 1981).

Richard, Yann, *Shi'ite Islam: Polity, Ideology and Creed*, tr. Antonia Nevill (Oxford (UK) and Cambridge (USA): Blackwell Publishers, 1995).

Rizvi, Sayyid Athar Abbas, *A Socio-Intellectual History of the Ithna-'Asharī Shī'īs in India*, i (Campbell, Australia: Ma'rifa Publishing House, 1986).

Rizvi, Sayyid Muhammad, *Marriage and Morals in Islam* (Winnipeg: Islamic Education Foundation, 1990).

Sābiq, Sayyid, *Fiqh Sunnah*, tr. Muhammed Sa'eed Dabas and Jamal al-Din M. Zarabozo (Indianapolis: American Trust Publications, n.d.).

al-Ṣāfī, Lutfullah, *Ma'al Khatīb fī Khutūtihi al-Arīḍah* (Tehran: n.p., 1987).

al-Shāfi'i, Muhammad ibn Idris, *al-Risālah fī Uṣūl al-Fiqh: Treatise on the Foundation of Islamic Jurisprudence* (Beirut: Dār al-Kutub al-'Ilmiyyah, n.d.).

al-Shahrastāni, Abdul-Karīm, *The Summa Philosophiae of al-Shahrastāni: Kitāb Nihāyatu 'I-Iqdām fī 'ilmi al-Kalām*, tr. and ed. Alfred Guillaume (Oxford: Oxford University Press, and London: Humphrey Milford, 1934).

al-Shahrazūrī, Ibn al-Ṣalāḥ *An Introduction to the Science of Hadith – Kitab Maʿrifat anwāʿ ʿilm al-Ḥadīth*, ed. Eerik Dickinson (Reading: Garnet Publishing Limited and Centre for Muslim Contribution to Civilization, 2006).

Sharif, Mohammad, *Innocently Accused* (Karachi: Islamic Seminary Publications, 1979).

Shomali, Mohammed A., *Shiʿi Islam: Origins, Faith & Practices* (London: Islamic College for Advanced Studies Press, 2003).

Siddiqi, Abdul Hamid, *Sahih Muslim*, tr. English (New Delhi: Kitab Bhavan, 2000).

Ṣiddīqī, Muhammad Zubayr, *Hadith Literature: Its Origin, Development and Special Features*, ed. Abdal Hakim Murad (Cambridge: Islamic Text Society, 1993).

Sobhani, Ayatollah Jaʿfar, *Doctrines of Shiʿi Islam: A Compendium of Imami Beliefs and Practices,* tr. Reza Shah-Kazemi (London and New York: I. B. Tauris Publishers, in association with the Institute of Ismaili Studies, 2001).

Sourdel, D., 'The Abbasid Caliphate', in P. M. Holt, Ann K. S. Lambton, and Bernard Lewis (eds.), *The Cambridge History of Islam* (Cambridge: Cambridge University, 1970).

Subhani, Jaʿfar, *The Message*, tr. Islamic Seminary (Tehran: Foreign Department of Be'that Foundation, 1984).

Tabatabā'ī, Muhammad Husayn, *Shi'ite Islam*, tr. and ed. Seyyed Hossein Nasr (London: George Allen & Unwin Ltd, 1975).

Tahir-ul-Qadri, Muhammad, *Fatwah on Terrorism and Suicide Bombings* (London: Minhaj-ul-Qur'an International, 2010).

University of Birmingham, *The Birmingham Qur'an Manuscript* (Birmingham: University of Birmingham, 2015).

Watt, William Montgomery, *The Formative Period of Islamic Thought* (Oxford: Oneworld Publications, 2002).

TRUE DIRECTIONS

An affiliate of Tarcher Perigee

OUR MISSION

Tarcher Perigee's mission has always been to publish books that contain great ideas. Why? Because:

GREAT LIVES BEGIN WITH GREAT IDEAS

At Tarcher Perigee, we recognize that many talented authors, speakers, educators, and thought-leaders share this mission and deserve to be published – many more than Tarcher Perigee can reasonably publish ourselves. True Directions is ideal for authors and books that increase awareness, raise consciousness, and inspire others to live their ideals and passions.

Like Tarcher Perigee, True Directions books are designed to do three things: inspire, inform, and motivate.

Thus, True Directions is an ideal way for these important voices to bring their messages of hope, healing, and help to the world.

Every book published by True Directions– whether it is non-fiction, memoir, novel, poetry or children's book – continues Tarcher Perigee's mission to publish works that bring positive change in the world. We invite you to join our mission.

For more information, see the True Directions website:

www.iUniverse.com/TrueDirections/SignUp

Be a part of Tarcher Perigee's community to bring positive change in this world! See exclusive author videos, discover new and exciting books, learn about upcoming events, connect with author blogs and websites, and more!
www.tarcherbooks.com

TRUE DIRECTIONS

AN AFFILIATE OF TARCHER PERIGEE

Printed in the United States
by Bookmasters

Printed in the United States
By Bookmasters